Malesherbes

From a portrait in the Chateau de Tocqueville

LAMOIGNON DE
MALESHERBES

DEFENDER AND REFORMER OF
THE FRENCH MONARCHY

1721–1794

BY

JOHN M. S. ALLISON

NEW HAVEN · YALE UNIVERSITY PRESS
London · Humphrey Milford · Oxford University Press
1938

Copyright, 1938, by Yale University Press

Printed in the United States of America

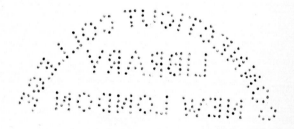

TO

M. L. M.

IN GRATITUDE AND AFFECTION

PREFACE

MALESHERBES *was not the foremost figure in France during the period immediately preceding the Revolution, but his career is significant as representative of an important class, the noblesse de robe, which played its part in preparing the way for the tragedy. In many ways, Malesherbes was a prophet of the Revolution. A liberal, he aided the philosophical movement in France, he assisted Turgot in trying to stem the tide of disaster, and he counseled the King. But his advice, although kindly received, was not followed. In the end, he returned from retirement and offered himself as one of the King's defenders. Ably he defended a hopeless cause, only a year later to pay the penalty of his loyalty at the guillotine.*

I am deeply indebted to the family of Tocqueville, the collateral descendants of the distinguished critic of American democracy, for their consideration and courtesy in placing at my disposal their entire collection of unpublished materials concerning their ancestor, Malesherbes. They have also taken the trouble to put me in touch with other documents relative to my subject. Without their friendly interest and encouragement it would have been impossible to complete this study. I regret to state that I have been unable to gain access to the papers of Malesherbes that are in the possession of the Marquis de Rosambo.

I owe as well an expression of gratitude to the descendants of Monsieur de Sèze, who delivered the plea for the King before the Convention. Through Professor Bernard Faÿ I was informed of a small but important collection of letters and manuscripts which are in the archives of Chateaurenard. To him, to Madame de Virel, the owner of Chateaurenard, and to Monsieur Paul Filleul, who has graciously forwarded me copies of these materials, I wish to express my deep appreciation. My thanks are also due to the Conservateur of the Bibliothèque Nationale and the Conservateur of the Archives Nationales for their courtesy in permitting me to use their collections. I wish to acknowledge as well the work of Mr. William B. Willcox and of Mr. Rynn Berry for help in making transcriptions.

To Mr. Geoffrey Merriss I owe a special debt of gratitude for his willing and invaluable assistance, his patience and fidelity. He has worked beside me both in this country and in France. Without his help this book could not have been done so easily or so pleasantly.

J. M. S. A.

July, 1937.

CONTENTS

ILLUSTRATIONS

MALESHERBES

CHAPTER I

THE BACKGROUND OF
CHRÉTIEN DE MALESHERBES

W HAT is necessary for my son if he is to succeed in life?" a noble parent inquired of his son's tutor. The Abbé replied: "He must learn to please, to be *aimable*. If he is *aimable,* he is sure of success."

In general this was the ideal of the class which, during the eighteenth century, was known as the *noblesse de l'épée,* the nobility of the Court and of the army. It surrounded the young King at Versailles, whose every wish was its law, and it formed a brilliant background against which the pageantry of the French monarchy was played off. This was not, however, the spirit and temper of the class to which Chrétien Lamoignon de Malesherbes belonged.

For one hundred and fifty years his family had been prominent members of the noblesse de robe, a powerful class of judges recently made hereditary and who presided over the sovereign courts and *parlements* of the realm. These magistrates stood halfway between the bourgeoisie and the nobility. They were close to the throne; some men even felt that they stood too close to it. Regarded with suspicion by the Court at Versailles, the members of the Parlement were a hard-working and a serious-minded lot. Their highest body was the Parlement of Paris which, with its seven chambers, had supervision over practically all matters concerning infringements of the law. Appeal could be made to it from the provincial parlements and tribunals. It alone had the right to register royal edicts and to demand a reconsideration of the laws that the King proposed to declare. Another tribunal, the Cour des Aides, had supervision over the collection of taxes and had the right of interpreting all ordinances that related to taxation. It is evident, then, that this class had come to possess a power which, at times, threatened even the privileges of the nobles and the will of the King.

Since the virtual abandonment of the Estates-General in 1614, the importance of the *parlementaires* had increased tenfold. Jealous of their own privileges and distinctions, even to the point of rebellion, they had come to regard themselves as a sort of national body. Their powers of remonstrance and of supervision of taxes gave them a certain claim to this pretension. They were, it is true, the only body through which the ordinary man in France could make himself heard by the King. In the opinion of many in the eighteenth century they were the guardians of the French people. But, in the beginning, that may have been simply because they were the zealous protectors of their own position in the face of King, councils, and nobles of the Court. The records of the Parlement are filled with petitions from merchants, farmers, and the steadily increasing number of men of business who appealed to one or another of its courts for relief and justice in their affairs. During the seventeenth century Parlement had actually, for a time, driven Mazarin and the young Louis XIV from Paris. More recently, they had asserted themselves in violent opposition to the policies of the Regent, the Duc d'Orléans, who had finally assumed the government in the name of the young King.

Consequently, in a sense, this class and its interests were more closely allied to the people of France than the King himself, enclosed as he was by the Court at Versailles and separated from his subjects by an army of administrators. The concerns of the parlementaires were wide; they had jurisdiction not only over most local courts, taxes, and commercial activities; they also had control over the censorship. They were a part of the monarchy and yet not a part of it, for they possessed, by tradition, the right to name their successors. They stood out in marked contrast to the rest of the nobility of France as a class not completely dependent upon the King. By the Court they were already regarded as revolutionaries, *philosophes,* Jansenists, whatever you will, whatever name will indicate a lack of conformity to the pattern of absolutism that flourished in this first part of the reign of Louis the Well-Beloved.

The great grandfather of Malesherbes had been first President of the Parlement in the time of Louis XIV. He had carried great weight in royal counsels and had been popularly known as "l'oracle de la Magistrature." He had been an elegant gentleman, the patron and friend of Boileau and Racine. Malesherbes' own father was at first head of the Parlement and later Chancellor of France. He was in many ways easygoing, and yet industrious and studious. Nevertheless Magistrate Lamoignon was not always taken seriously. D'Argenson wrote of him in his journal: "He is a good magistrate, not much enlightened, and with little imagination; a huge stomach, an enormous appetite, much beloved by the Jesuits who have made him." He was a far different person from his elegant forbear. In many ways, he was more conservative than the Court. He was a strict puritan, and he avoided Versailles as much as possible because he felt out of place there. Of such a conventional parent Chrétien Lamoignon de Malesherbes was born on December 6, 1721.

Early in his life it was decided that the young son should follow in the footsteps of his father. In the beginning his parents had visions of making him an officer in the army or a courtier as his ancestor had been. But these plans were dissipated when the family dancing master reported that the son would never learn to dance well and that, therefore, he could not succeed in the army or at the Court. The best thing to do, he said, would be to prepare him for the Church. At this suggestion the disappointed father rebelled, and a family council finally decreed that the son and heir should follow the career of a magistrate. From the time of this decision, great care was taken of his education. At first he was placed under a priestly tutor at the family estate. Later he was sent to Paris, lodged with his grandmother, and taken in charge by the Abbé Pucelle, nephew of the late powerful Maréchal de Catinat. Under the guidance of this Abbé and a subsequent tutor, the Abbé Radonvilliers, Malesherbes was instructed in the classics, in history, and in jurisprudence. This program, however, represented only one half of his preparation for life.

Like the other members of the noblesse de robe, President Lamoignon possessed lands. His largest estate was in the Orléanais near Pithiviers. These lands were worked to the limit for the income that they brought, and they were already famed for the beauty of their gardens and for the quantity of game found in their woods. The young Malesherbes must learn to manage these estates. And so to his legal and historical studies there was added the study of account books, titles, land resources, and management of the tenantry. During the spring and autumn the son devoted himself to learning the concerns of a country gentleman. He is said to have applied himself with great diligence and with evident enjoyment. In later years, Malesherbes became a noted authority on farming methods and on botany; his earlier experience undoubtedly aroused his first enthusiasm for this sort of occupation.

The remainder of his time, when the fields were idle, was spent in study in Paris. There, in the capital, life was not exciting. All the world of high society flocked to Versailles. Writers state that Paris was left almost entirely to the bourgeois and the solemn parlementaires. Malesherbes' days, according to a contemporary, were passed in "meeting judges, in reading great legal tomes, and in remarkably few, if any, indiscretions."

There was little in this environment to predict Malesherbes of the Cour des Aides, the friend of the philosophes, the jovial raconteur, the devoted adherent of reform under Turgot, and, at the end, the fearless old man who dared to defend his King. This was a dismal setting for a young man of spirit. A rigid puritanism, and a cold, almost classic reserve animated the circle to which his family belonged. The slightest deviation from its established code brought a stern rebuke. Once Malesherbes took part in an escapade with a group of medical students. The irate magistrate, his father, recalled to him the dignity of the profession upon which he was entering. There are no other evidences of lapses from the strict code of behavior which was generally observed by the magistrature. Life continued monotonously and virtuously. At the early age of twenty-one he became a substitute under the Procureur General of the Parlement in Paris, and, in July, 1744, he was received as a counselor at the Parlement. His first discourses before that body made an excellent impression.

A few years later fortune blazed upon the family of Malesherbes. In 1750 the father was made Chancellor of France, and, in the same year, the son was appointed First President of the Cour des Aides and then Director of the Librairie, a nomination made by his father. As President of the Cour des Aides, Malesherbes became concerned with all matters relating to taxation; as Director of the Librairie he was virtually in charge of the censorship in France. More important for his future, however, was the temper of France in the year 1750. When Malesherbes assumed these posts, France was just entering upon the critical phase of her political and intellectual experience.

ALMOST six years to the day before the birth of Malesherbes, the reign of Louis XIV came to an inglorious close. With the passing of the King, even before it, the unity of the ancien régime had begun to break down.

The seventeenth century had a mania for unity. Colbert and his organization of political and economic life, Vauban with his military policy, the Church with its drastic measures against dissent, and the Academies with their dictatorship over letters and arts, all had united to enclose France within an exclusive and perfect system. The nation should be homogeneous and self-sufficient. French system, French taste, French art had come under such a sway and, for a

time, they had ruled the world. It had been the belief of
the late King that this unity and this predominance would
continue after his time. But even before his death cracks
had appeared in the magnificent surface of French superi-
ority and prosperity. France ceased to be self-sufficient and
lost her apparent complacency. Colbert's system had at first
succeeded and then it had failed; Vauban's organization
had gone down to defeat before the Allies during the War
of the Spanish Succession; while libertinage in letters and
in political thought had begun to make itself felt. The
world of the ancien régime was passing and was making
way for a new regime as diverse as the seventeenth century
had been homogeneous, more tolerant, and, above all, more
cosmopolitan.

Jesuit teachers and the dictates of French classicism had
closed the doors to foreign influence during most of the century of Louis XIV, but toward its close new and unexpected
results of this practice of exclusion became evident. France
was weary of sameness. Frenchmen began to look beyond
their own frontiers, to travel, and to question their own system. Noble and lettered society could not exist forever in
the precious atmosphere of the salons of Paris. The French
mind could not develop and French style could not flourish
perpetually on the traditions of classicism. Unconsciously,
at first, Frenchmen began to form foreign contacts, to study
foreign languages and literature, and, in this fashion, to
meet with foreign thought.

The seventeenth century had scarcely ended and the
eighteenth century begun when travel companies, literary
clubs, and foreign journals became the rage in the country.
England, then Germany, and finally Switzerland began to
make their impress on France. Translations became popu-

lar. The records of the Librairie show that, within the first
three decades of the new century, permits were granted for
twenty translations from the Spanish, fifty-two from the
Italian, seventy-six from the German, and two hundred and
forty-five from the English. Even more surprising was the
appearance of new journals that treated of foreign affairs
and criticism. Among the more popular of them were the
Journal encyclopédique, the *Journal des savants* edited by
the Abbé Bignon, and the *Journal étranger* that was later
published under the direction of the Abbé Arnaud and
patronized by the Duc de Choiseul, minister of the King.

At the same time, clubs for the discussion of foreign
news and foreign culture were formed. Abbé Alary, tutor
to the royal children, founded in 1721 the Club de l'Entresol. This society had twenty members. It subscribed to a
number of foreign papers. At its biweekly meetings the
members discussed the news of the gazettes, the fate of
Poland, and the government of Switzerland. At one time
they actually embarked upon a study of the history of the
Estates-General. One of its members, the Abbé de Saint-
Pierre, presented to his colleagues a plan for perpetual in-
ternational peace. The club had foreign members and corre-
spondents. Among them were the Scotchman Ramsay,
Bolingbroke, and Robert Walpole. Later royal censorship
became alarmed and the club was closed. After that some
of its former members went occasionally to London, where,
at the Rainbow Tavern, they encountered the intellectuals
of England. Gradually, salons, too, took on this cosmopolitan character, and several of them, notably that of Madame
du Deffand, became centers for the dissemination of this
spirit.

Out of these contacts and interests, of which the Entresol

is but one example, came a renewed enthusiasm for travel, for science, and for nature. The diversities of climates, physical environment, and customs began to fascinate the educated world. Abbé Prêvot published in 1728 his *Histoire générale des voyages* in twenty volumes. The works of Cook went through several French editions. More profound study was represented by Buffon's *Histoire naturelle,* in which the author attempted to present the entire physical history of the globe from the time when it was a mass of burning lava to his own day. A little later came Montesquieu's *Lettres Persanes,* which purported to turn the eyes of the oriental on occidental manners and environment. The realization of the diversities that existed about them led Frenchmen to investigate and to compare the rest of the world with their own part of it.

This intense mania for nature inspired, above all, a deep concern about Man and the society that he had built in other parts of the world. Where was Man happiest? Where was he the most free? Answers were as varied as the societies and customs that they found. French society became composed of Anglophiles, Germanophiles, and, of course, of those who idealized the American Quaker or the man on the American frontier. Sometimes their enthusiasms carried them to greater lengths. There was the cult of the Gentle Savage whose devotees raved over the American Indian or the Tahitian and attributed to them all of the virtues and none of the vices of their own more elegant civilization. Even more popular, in Paris, was the interest in the Common Man. Diderot extolled him and Greuze with his brush depicted his homely and righteous existence. Even the theater took him up and presented such mawkish plays as *The Good Father.* Society wished to study him close at

hand, and *sociétés de bienfaisance* made polite expeditions
to observe him on his farm or in his workshop. This organized curiosity spread, it seems, a superficial sentiment
of good will which affected many of the members of higher
society in France during the eighteenth century. And it
brought developments that were far more robust and far
more sincere. This mild spirit of inquiry prepared the way
for the more trenchant criticism of the philosophes which
made the latter part of the century an age devoted to the
merciless assessment of the past and a preparation for a
totally new future.

Across the Channel from England and over the frontiers
from Holland and Germany came a new science and a new
philosophy. France was deluged with a new spirit of inquiry and criticism. Locke's doctrines upset many of the
prevalent ideas of the time and threatened the very bases of
revealed religion, while Newton's experiments and laws
challenged the whole approach to established knowledge
and science. There were Frenchmen, too, who in exile had
published their doubts and then smuggled them across the
frontiers into France. Pierre Bayle began by questioning the
prophetical significance of comets and then brought out his
Dictionnaire critique, which set up beside Descartes' Law of
Reason his own Commandment of Doubt. Fontenelle's
Histoire des oracles had attacked many prevalent super-
stitions.

These were the currents of thought that prevailed in
France toward the close of the epoch of Louis XIV and during the first part of the reign of his successor. Doubt, tolerance, and the abhorrence of ignorance became the new doctrines of the day. Reform of society, readjustment of rights
and privileges, and social equality became watchwords.

Many of those who had received their education in the Jesuit schools now became the eager disciples of a new intellectual dispensation that was just beginning to take form. It lacked as yet coherence and unity, but it afforded a totally new outlook on the past and the promise of an adventurous future. Some of these apostles believed that a new civilization was at their very doors that would bring with it a new religion, a new liberty, and a greater science. For that, there would have to be a new basis of knowledge and a complete abandonment of the traditions of the more recent past. Diderot, D'Alembert, and Helvetius envisaged the creation of another Summa of knowledge, an encyclopedia that would serve as the foundation for a new world.

It was these projects of the philosophes that brought to the fore Malesherbes, the young Director of the Librairie.

CHAPTER II

MALESHERBES AND THE
PHILOSOPHES

THE appointment of Malesherbes as head of the Librairie almost coincided in point of time with his marriage. His bride, Marie Françoise Grimaud de la Reynière, came of an old family long distinguished in the history of Paris. As was customary, the marriage had been arranged by the families of the young couple, but it resulted, nevertheless, from an affair of the heart. A generous income was provided for them, and their situation was further improved by the grant of a pension of a thousand livres a year from the King.

Madame de Malesherbes afforded a contrast in interests and in character to her husband. She was active, fond of outdoor life, a splendid horsewoman, and passionately devoted to hunting. Malesherbes already preferred his study, a strong pipe, his botany and his gardens, and the telling of a good story. In spite of these differences, perhaps even because of them, the union was at first a happy one. An able mistress of her husband's household, Madame de Malesherbes won general approval as the hostess of the charming house where they established themselves in the Quartier du Marais, in Paris, convenient to the Palais de Justice.

When Malesherbes set up his household and assumed his official duties, his opinions and his intelligence were well formed. The study and pursuit of the law had not been allowed to prevent his cultivating polite literature.

He was acquainted with most of the ancient and modern classics. His friends relate that he quoted Horace, Virgil, and Ovid as often as Corneille and Racine. La Fontaine was his great favorite. Nature-lover and fond of satire as Malesherbes was, he reveled in the anecdotes of the poet. Molière's wit, he wrote, was an inspiration. The young Malesherbes was already an acute but kindly observer of the society he found about him. In other words, he fulfilled the requirements of the average gentlemen of the eighteenth century. But he had gone even a little beyond them: his own intellectual merit had been recognized by his election to the Académie des Sciences. And, within a short while, he would be made a member of the Académie des Inscriptions et Belles Lettres.

Like many another Frenchman of his rank and age, who was both country gentleman and man of profession in Paris, Malesherbes was not prepared to follow slavishly the conventions and beliefs of his parents and forbears. He had already read many of the advanced writers of his time. He was acquainted with Montesquieu and had dipped into Voltaire. Through French authors he had come in touch with the ideas of Locke and Newton. He had been carried away with enthusiasm by the Abbé de Saint-Pierre's book on foreign lands and travel, and had already begun a collection of travel books of his own. He had also studied with interest the works of Pierre Bayle. Malesherbes himself acknowledged that it was Bayle who planted in his mind the first seed of skepticism. In brief, he had come into the heritage of eighteenth-century ideas and had been slightly influenced by them. He liked to call himself at this time a moderate disciple of the new philosophy which, in his own fashion, he described as follows:

"The philosophy which I profess, my friend, is the one that wisdom teaches us—love of truth, love of our fellow men, obedience to the laws, and exactitude in fulfilling the duties of a good father, a good husband, an honest man, and a true citizen."

This is not the conventional understanding of the word philosophy as it is applied today to the eighteenth century. It expresses, nevertheless, what was often a very real part of the eighteenth-century concept—humanitarianism and reason. Even, one might say, in the case of Malesherbes, it was humanitarianism checked by reason. In an unpublished commentary on Montesquieu, Malesherbes wrote: "I tell you that by the word philosophe I mean followers of the true philosophy, namely, those who are without ambition and who have no other desire than to see a reasonable liberty."

His orthodoxy was already hardly more than formal. It was even questioned by some of his contemporaries. At a later time Louis XVI, in the midst of his danger, remarked to Malesherbes: "Ah, Monsieur de Malesherbes, if you only had a stronger faith in God." It is significant that Malesherbes appears to have let the remark pass without comment. Although he never formally renounced the Catholic religion, he was a freethinker, and he stood firmly and solidly for religious toleration. This was the state of his mind in matters of philosophy and religion—a mild skeptic.

What Malesherbes could not endure was ignorant belief: "One should enlighten all men; ignorance is the source of most of our faults. It is the established people, the lords of parishes, the curés, the priests, who wish the people to be ignorant—all the interested ones desire it, and they

are therefore suspect." Malesherbes mistrusted those who
approved of leaving the people in ignorance. To him, their
attitude implied that they were not persuaded of the truth
of their own beliefs. "On est si sûr de persuader quand on
l'est soi-même. The Abbé de Fleuri once remarked that religion should never fear to be examined." Again, he abominated the idea of a privileged clergy and the close alliance
of Church and State. In this same commentary on Montesquieu he wrote: "Why is the clergy an order, and the first
order in the State? By the very nature of things, the clergy
should be simple *pensionnaires* of the State, as the tutor of
the house. Those who have dogmas and maxims of the
other world may preach them, but they may not govern
this world. Because of its very nature the clergy favors despotism, for the character of religion is passive obedience—
and [that is known] only too well in England."

It was the reading of Fénelon that first presented to him
the idea of political and social reform. There were many
well-intentioned people in France who had been deeply affected by the mild and rather platitudinous humanitarianism of Fénelon, whose influence had been greatest toward
the end of the reign of Louis XIV. Malesherbes had inherited this line of thought from his tutors, and he had
been struck by the obvious sincerity of Fénelon's *Télémaque*. Once he had exclaimed: "There is the book of
kings, of ministers, and of all those who govern. . . . All
the duties of the various classes of society are outlined there
in letters of gold; all is electrified by the pen of Fénelon.
With him all takes on a body and a soul."

In accord with Fénelon's ideas, Malesherbes and his
friends believed in a benevolent monarchy more powerful
than the present one, which was obstructed by the nobles

and favorites. They sought to reform the nobility, to give it a useful place in the life of the nation, and to create among all classes a sense of mutual obligations and duties. But even this early in his life Malesherbes carried Fénelon's thought a little further, and he envisaged the equalization of all burdens, especially taxes, among all classes of the nation. At this time he thought, even, of the reconciliation of France by allowing its citizens a part in the government. Although he was a parlementaire, as early as 1756 he was talking of a National Assembly which might have a greater authority than the courts of Parlement.

To these moderately advanced ideas with which he began his public life, one other interest should be added. Almost every educated man of the eighteenth century had begun to develop the hobby of science or nature study. Paris was amusing itself with all forms of mild scientific investigation. Philosophers, nobles, and bishops were playing at it in their private laboratories or by attending meetings of societies devoted to the study of magnetism, physics, and astronomy. Chemistry and botany had become so popular that they were introduced into the curricula of seminaries for young ladies of fashion. Even the pulpits were given over to science; it was a common although perhaps somewhat exaggerated saying that the only mention of faith that was heard during the average sermon in Paris was the invocation of the Holy Trinity at the beginning.

On first coming to Paris as a student, Malesherbes had joined a medical society. It is said that he attended almost as many lectures on medicine as on the law. He devoured eagerly the scientific pamphlets of Réaumur, Montesquieu, and D'Alembert. A country gentleman to the core, how-

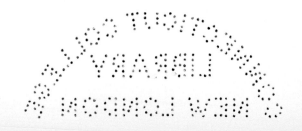

ever, it was naturally in botany that he found his greatest
delight.

When he was staying on the estate near Pithiviers, he
would work late into the night. He nearly impaired his
eyesight studying Linnæus. When Buffon appeared to re-
fute the Linnæan categories, it was Malesherbes who set
about to destroy the author of the *Histoire naturelle*. The
lands at Malesherbes became the scene of experiments of
all sorts where rare plants and trees, arranged according to
their proper categories, were grown. There he tried out
new methods for fertilizing the soil. When the experiments gave promise of success, the news was spread and
the tenantry and other landlords of the neighborhood
came to see the result. In the archives at Tocqueville there
are a quantity of notes and reports on experiments written
in the fine, almost illegible hand of Malesherbes. There are
also copies of letters to English seed merchants ordering
rare specimens. At a later time he arranged, through fellow countrymen who had gone to America, for the im-
portation of native plants from the Carolinas and from
Florida and Virginia. He added to his library on travel and
foreign lands, particularly in the New World. He delighted in the tales of travelers and their observations on
the habits of other races, on native products and climates.
Some of his collection was not even printed material, but
manuscript copies made by his secretaries from the original
accounts.

These months spent in the country, while the courts of
Parlement were not in session, became times of anxiety
for his family, because Malesherbes made them periods of
intense study. At night, clad in an old brown woolen robe,

a white cap on his head, and his feet in heavy felt slippers, he was accustomed to sit at his desk for hours going over his notes in preparation for the *Herbier*. It is related that twice he worked so late and took so little notice of the chill night air that he came down with pneumonia and his life was despaired of. When the chancellor was informed of these goings-on in the provinces he shrugged his shoulders and raised his eyes to heaven in sign of his failure to comprehend such a son.

The fact was that this new generation would not be as the older one had been, and Malesherbes, with this multitude of new ideas and new interests about him would not be such a censor or such a magistrate as his predecessors had been. In both roles he became one of the earliest prophets of the Revolution.

THE Department of the Librairie had jurisdiction over all matters relating to printing and publication. This included control·and censorship of newspapers, journals, and books within France as well as literary importations from foreign lands.

When Malesherbes assumed the title of Directeur Général de la Librairie et de l'Imprimerie the condition of the book trade was not a flourishing one. The market was glutted with foreign importations. The censorship was too strict, and the privileges of publication were too infrequently granted. As in industry, certain corporations had practically monopolized the trade, and there was little inducement to new enterprises. The interference of petty functionaries and their practice of arbitrary inspection not only of printers' shops but even of printers' houses intimidated and discouraged publication. Popular, sprightly, and provocative writing when done by Frenchmen usually had to be published in foreign lands and gotten, by some means, across the frontiers into France. This situation Malesherbes exposed in detail to the King but only after he had made a careful examination of the laws and practices of other countries: "The book trade today is too general and the public demands too great, for us to be able to maintain these restrictions beyond a certain point, for a taste for reading is dominant in the country. . . . And we should grant more liberty to the press. . . . It is already far greater in Holland, in Switzerland, and in the Protestant states of Germany." This was his way of stating to the King what he had already expressed to his friends in stronger terms. "What is important is that the truth be made known. There are only two really good reasons for prohibiting a book; when an author has dared to submit royal authority to examination and when an author has expressed sentiments that would tend to lower public morals and religion."

His enemies have asserted that Malesherbes was interested only in the commercial aspect of the problem and that he would do anything to increase the business of book-selling and publishing. It is true that at the outset all his efforts were directed to this end and that he gained the hostility of the older established corporations by encouraging new enterprises in the provinces as well as in Paris. Nevertheless, it is significant that in the Archives de la Librairie there are not only a quantity of new licenses issued in this period but also a great deal of correspondence

containing advice for the new publishers on the standards
and quality that were expected of them. Malesherbes was
eager for France to regain her place in the republic of letters. Frequently when he approved a refusal to license a
book or paper the sole reason was that it was poorly written or vulgar. For a time, for example, he allowed the
Journal étranger a free hand not because it was patronized
by the Duc de Choiseul but "because," he writes, "its in-
vention and plan attracted all France, and it was without
a doubt the most useful and commendable paper that the
nation had." But when it became cheap and sensational
Malesherbes himself was instrumental in prohibiting it.
He was not afraid of innovations, and so he permitted the
appearance of a work by one Monsieur Bernard, which
bore the ominous title *Projet d'un nouvel état de la France*.
In fact, he even assisted Bernard in obtaining permission
to utilize materials in private libraries. In 1762 he tried to
recall the maps and geographies still on sale in Paris in
order to have them brought up to date and into accord
with the most recent discoveries.

Form, precision of language, and quality of content
were the three criteria that he was constantly demanding
of authors and publishers. Even in the case of doubtful
books he would not always trust the unfavorable verdict
of the person whom he had appointed to read them. On
frequent occasions he undertook to examine a book that
had been condemned and then himself canceled the verdict of the censor whom he had named. This was exactly
what happened in the case of D'Holbach's translation of
letters on science from the German. Such a freedom and
consideration was introduced into the Department of the
Librairie as had not been known before in France, and it

was grace that was equally distributed among high and low.

As censor Malesherbes was not influenced by the social status or popularity of a reader or author. When the Duc d'Orléans imported, as was most like him, a case of literary trash, the matter was reported to the director by his agent at the port. The director informed Monseigneur that he would allow the box to pass but that he did not approve of his taste. He even took Voltaire to task for certain expressions. This action the patriarch never entirely forgot, although Malesherbes gave him considerable assistance when he was collecting his material for the writing of *The Age of Louis XIV*. Voltaire was practically the only one of the philosophes with whom Malesherbes was not on very friendly terms, but even he acknowledged that the director had fought great battles for the cause of the *gens de lettres* in France. By most of them Malesherbes was regarded as a friend, firm and sympathetic, although cautious. By a few this caution was condoned as a family trait inherited from his father, the chancellor; others realized that Malesherbes was by no means the complete master of his department and that he must act with care and circumspection.

Not the least of the difficulties which he encountered were found among the authors whose friend and protector he tried to be. At one and the same time he was their confidant and the battleground for their *amours-propres,* their personal jealousies, and their petty animosities. Even the greater philosophes were constantly squabbling among themselves. Often Malesherbes was made the victim of their peculiarities and personal whims. But he bore with these people patiently: "I have at last become accustomed to the cajoleries, petty animosities, and fits of temper to which men of letters are subject; now I am rarely offended by their actions, for I have learned that these little faults are inseparable from their talents."

In the beginning, he was astonished by the strange and unreasonable prejudices which he met among the censors and magistrates. Their objections were not always based on the grounds of religion and morality. Frequently they were founded on that uncertain and fickle principle which is called taste. "I have actually heard people seriously assert that it is wrong to allow any music except Italian to be printed, for, they say, Italian is the only good music. I know magistrates who regard it as an abuse of the law to permit the publication of elementary works on jurisprudence, on the ground that these books will diminish the number of real savants. Most physicians prefer to prohibit works on medicine written in the vulgar tongue, and all those who have played a part in public life dislike to see authors writing on politics, commerce, and legislation."

Sometimes, too, he encountered opposition even from his family. His father, the chancellor, a friend of the Jesuits, did not fail, at intervals, to take issue with his son and condemn permissions which the director had granted. On one occasion, their disagreement was so great that the son threatened to resign his post with the Librairie and declared that he was entirely disillusioned by "this painful lesson on the arbitrary and useless character of the censorship."

As Director of the Librairie and Imprimerie, he must observe caution and tact if his philosophical friends were to enjoy the privilege of having their works published or distributed within the country. Every new book or journal was submitted to the director. He then appointed a special reader for it. When the reader's report was received, the director issued a license, or refused it, or demanded alterations. But in some cases, even if approval were given by the director, publication was not assured. It might be stopped by a decree of the King's council, by an order of Parlement, or else an offended party, who had the royal ear, might obtain a *lettre de cachet* and send the author to Vincennes or to the Bastille. In 1748 Diderot had that sad experience when his famous *Letter on the Blind* appeared.

In such instances even the director did not escape without a severe reprimand: "Sir, the vice-chancellor has instructed me to write you and to urge you to redouble your attention and care in the matter of the censorship. When you find in books which have been submitted to your department passages concerning religion or the government, you should render me a detailed account before giving your approval to them. It is also his intention that you send me more detailed reasons for your approbations and that you indicate more precisely the character of the books which you are examining."

Malesherbes' efforts as director required considerable diplomacy and often necessitated negotiations with other and more conservative elements in the government. Sometimes it was even necessary to negotiate with the King. If all else failed he had been known to resort to a tacit permission and to allow the book to be printed without any special authorization, even making it appear that it had come from another country. In most of these affairs the director displayed an adroitness that was not untouched with guile. The affair of Helvetius is a case in point.

During the spring of 1758 Helvetius submitted the

manuscript of *De l'Esprit humain*. No sooner had he sent it to Malesherbes than he took alarm and wrote to him: "I am overwhelmed by your kindness and I rely always on your friendship. I hope, indeed, that you have not appointed a theologian to read my book." This was actually what Malesherbes had done, for the book was a study in which the author had ascribed all human endeavor to utilitarian motives. On the recommendation of the first reader, publication was delayed. At Helvetius' request Malesherbes himself then read the book. He found it so entertaining that he wrote the reverend gentleman who had acted as censor that he considered his objections of no account. He then saw the King about it, but Louis XV, influenced by the Jesuits, refused to grant the license. At once, Malesherbes set out to find an important patron for Helvetius. His search was successful when the Duchesse d'Orléans agreed to undertake the matter. Thereupon Malesherbes appointed another reader, the Abbé de Bernis, who was more liberally inclined than his predecessor had been. Finally through the combined efforts of Malesherbes, De Bernis, and the Duchesse, the book of Helvetius was licensed *avec privilège du roi,* that is, by special permission. Only a few deletions were made, and the volume was published. Defeat, however, was in the offing. Within a few days, the Sorbonne condemned the book, and the King's privilege was revoked. Much the same sort of procedure was followed in regard to the works of D'Alembert and of the liberal Abbé Morellet. In these instances, Malesherbes was more successful.

The most difficult problem of all was presented by the Encyclopedia. Even before its appearance Diderot and D'Alembert, the directors of the enterprise, found them-

selves at grips with the Court and the Church. Foreseeing
a storm, D'Alembert betook himself to Malesherbes. Two
interviews assured him not only of the sympathy of Malesherbes but also of the approval of Madame de Pompadour,
who was later to contribute an article on "Rouge." The
Encyclopedia was formally announced in a prospectus
written by Diderot. The *Discours préliminaire,* a remarkable bit of synthesis treating the progress of human intelligence, was done by D'Alembert.

From the very moment when this important project first
became known, Church, Jesuits, and Court took alarm.
The move for the Encyclopedia revealed to them the fact
that now the philosophers were animated by a sense of confidence and unity of purpose. The array of contributors was
too imposing to suit the taste of the reactionaries. It included
some of the best known and ablest writers of the day; Voltaire, Montesquieu, Rousseau, D'Holbach, Morellet, Helvetius, Quesnay, Turgot, and Condorcet were among those
who were expected to contribute articles. The opinions of
these men were, by this time, well known. Churchmen
and Jesuits saw a concerted attack on the whole fabric of
knowledge that they had been at such pains to construct.
They looked with fear and horror upon these philosophers
who dared to assert that there was nothing that would remain unknown, that there was no mystery which Reason
could not make plain. Men of the government ridiculed
and yet feared the doctrine that Reason would reveal a science of governing and a system of society far better than
the present ones. Many of them did not wish the people of
France to hear any more of this cant about "a more righteous and a freer world." Even more alarming, to their
minds, was the avowed purpose of the Encyclopedists.

They did not intend to limit their work to a simple protest against absolute monarchy, the regime of privilege,
and the abuses of the Catholic religion. It was their firm
belief that the Encyclopedia would lay the foundations for
an entirely new civilization by bringing together "all that
had been discovered in science, all that was known of the
products of the world, the details of the arts which men
have invented, the principles of morals and of legislation,
all laws which govern society, the metaphysics of language
and grammar, the analysis of our faculties, and the history
of our ideas and opinions." It was to be a great work assess-
ing the past and in which the assessment and acceptance
of the new world were to be coördinated and completed.
In itself, the Encyclopedia was a revolution.

By January, 1752, two volumes had appeared. It was
after the publication of the second volume that the watch-
dogs of the old regime arose en masse. The Abbé de
Prades, a friend of Diderot and a contributor to the Encyclopedia, delivered at the Sorbonne a discourse on Gene-
sis in which he questioned the chronology and appeared to
cast doubt on miracles. Then it was that the battle began.
The discourse was shortly condemned by the learned doc-
tors, and this verdict was followed by an avalanche of epis-
copal pastorals warning the faithful of the menace that
roamed the shops and bookstalls and calling for the silenc-
ing of De Prades, Montesquieu, and Diderot and his as-
sistants. Malesherbes came at once to their defense. But for
a moment it looked as if the cause of the Encyclopedists
was lost. From the pulpits they were denounced as disciples of the English heretics Bacon, Newton, and Locke.
Even Fréron led his fellow publishers, who were conservatives, in an attack and printed bitter diatribes in which

he described Voltaire, Diderot, and all the group as *co-quins, fripons,* and *scélérats.* Apparently, monarchy itself became convinced that some concession should be made to the outraged feelings of the *Dévôts,* and on February 7, 1752, a decree of the King's council was issued. This law forbade the publishers to reprint the first two volumes and ordered the confiscation of what remained of them. There was, however, a significant omission in the law: thanks to the personal intervention of the Director of the Librairie, the decree made no mention one way or the other of the continuance of the work.

This was Malesherbes' first stroke for the cause of Diderot and his companions. At once he took in hand the matter of the succeeding volumes. He even threatened the editors before he told them that they might proceed: "There you have my intention. I can impose obstacles on men of letters, confound their genius, complain of the faults that they commit, and I have not yet any favor that I can procure for them: but you must promise to allow nothing to appear that would offend the government."

At the request of the director, D'Alembert undertook to edit and write the Preface for the third volume. It appeared in November, 1753. Into the Preface D'Alembert put a splendid defense of Diderot and himself. It concluded on a note of bitterness that further irritated his enemies: "Let us recall the fable of Bocalini: 'A traveler was disturbed by the chirruping of grasshoppers, he sought to slay every one and was delayed and missed his way; he need only have gone peacefully along, and the grasshoppers would have died before the week was out.' "

The storm over the Encyclopedia subsided for a time. Diderot and D'Alembert continued their work. Male-

sherbes watched over them carefully. He encouraged
Diderot to continue his articles on the arts and industries.
Sometimes, to their annoyance, he pointed out lapses in
their treatment and chided them occasionally for omissions. When D'Alembert was elected to the Academy,
Malesherbes rejoiced in the event and saw in it the victory
of the Encyclopedists. But in this opinion he was mistaken.
Again, in 1758, the agitation against them was renewed,
and Parlement appointed a commission to investigate the
matter. The result was a second decree from the royal
council in March, 1759. D'Alembert complained to Morellet, who had become a firm friend of Malesherbes, that
the director was responsible for allowing the Jesuits to re-
new their attack. After many interviews, Malesherbes set
forth in a brief the principles of his administration. In this
astonishing letter he laid down the right that the citizen
had to criticize publicly the acts of administrators like
himself. As to literary criticism, he averred, if you allow
liberty, you must allow argument and even attack. Freedom of opinion and tolerance were necessary for all men
who engaged in literary or philosophical pursuits. This letter mollified D'Alembert. In the end, the law was allowed
to become a dead letter, and the work was resumed through
the efforts of Malesherbes, Madame de Pompadour, and
Choiseul, the King's minister.

In the Encyclopedia there was inserted an article entitled "Librairie." It was written by Diderot. A part of this
article read: "Under the new auspices of Monsieur de
Malesherbes, the Librairie changed its complexion and
took on a new form and a new vigor: the trade grew and
increased rapidly, so much so that now greater enterprises
are undertaken. . . . We acknowledge here with gratitude

what we owe to his kindness. It is to this magistrate, himself a lover of science and a faithful scholar, that France
owes this inspiration which he gave and which he fosters
every day among men of learning, an inspiration which
has brought forth so many excellent and profound works."

To this sentiment even Voltaire, who had long since
abandoned the Encyclopedists as too radical a group, uttered a fervent Amen. Quite different, however, was the
opinion of the defeated opposition, some of whom in 1790
blamed Malesherbes for the Revolution, because he had
protected the Encyclopedists and had made possible the
spread of the new learning of the eighteenth century.

From the time of the crisis over the Encyclopedia Malesherbes was regarded as the most powerful agent of the
government on behalf of the philosophes. But he was never
really their agent, although he was always their friend and
protector. Fearless of criticism of himself, he believed that
criticism should be welcomed and unrestricted. "Why
not," he asked, "censure that which has been established
when it is evil and harmful?" Criticism was only dangerous when it was restricted and, therefore, secret.

Nevertheless, there were points where Malesherbes was
not in accord with many of the writers whom he had
known and protected during this period of office as Director of the Librairie. He abominated a certain amount of
the philosophic jargon of his century: "Would that writers
would cease using such worn-out expressions as 'placed between the throne and the people.' . . . I have no idea what
is meant by the phrase 'put philosophy on the throne.'
*Trois quarts de ces philosophes sur le trône seraient des
philosophes de rez-de-chaussée.*" He had no sympathy
with the cult of the bourgeoisie which some of the writ-

ers were extolling—to the end he remained an aristocrat.
"I do not see that trade is respectable. It is good, and it
should be protected. But how can the occupation of buying
and selling be respectable? If only the philosophers did not
exaggerate." In his eyes the bourgeois was frequently as
selfish as the noble. Consequently, he had little use for the
idea of a republic: "Few republics," he wrote in his *Commentary on Montesquieu*, "have been established from a
conviction of equality and the advantages which it brings;
they have been born of a hatred of tyranny. . . . Republi-
cans love their republic as monks love their convent. Their
inability to amount to anything as individuals makes them
attach themselves to a corps in order, by it and with it, to
amount to something." Unlike many of his contemporaries, he believed that national happiness was more important than national strength. He expressed an extreme dislike for Montesquieu's admiration of the victories of Rome.
"If they would but teach the people that their real interest
lies in peace, that it makes little difference whether the
boundaries of their empire are wide or narrow. If only
they are happy and if only scheming and ambitious men
do not seduce them, the motives of glory and grandeur
will not drag them into foolish enterprises."

These opinions may be said to represent the negative
side of Malesherbes' philosophy at the beginning of the
last year of his tenure as Director of the Librairie. On the
other hand, there was a positive side which accounts in
great part for the fact that current opinion at the Court had
come to regard him as a revolutionary. It will be seen that
he supported wholeheartedly the ideas of financial reform,
the abolition of privilege, and a policy of religious tolera-

tion. In short, he participated in most of the important humanitarian aspects of eighteenth-century thought.

Before his dismissal as director, he presented a second petition to the King urging greater liberty for the press and the abandonment of the heavy restrictions set upon foreign works. Voltaire's comment is typical as well as significant: "Monsieur de Malesherbes has rendered infinite services to human genius by giving a greater liberty to the press than it has ever known before—we are already more than half Englishmen."

This from Voltaire, who rarely forgot or forgave chastisement, was indeed praise.

CHAPTER III

MALESHERBES AND ROUSSEAU
AN EPISODE

You ask me if your misfortunes have chilled my esteem and my friendship for you. These things were of concern only to those whom your works have inspired with a moderate admiration. . . . For myself, I have always loved and admired in you that spirit of truth so strong, courageous, and passionately virtuous which pervades all your writing. It is true, I have not adopted all of your sentiments even in regard to small matters, and, to still greater degree, I have found myself at odds with you in regard to the most important principles which you have discussed in your more recent works.

At all times I have blamed or rather regretted your imprudence in expressing yourself on everything without *ménagement*. There, Monsieur, you have what I always thought of you before your misfortunes. Judge now for yourself whether they have been able to make me change.

MALESHERBES *to* ROUSSEAU *at Montmorency, 13 November, 1762.*

IN his relations with the philosophers Malesherbes had been friendly but always brutally frank. This was also true in the case of Rousseau, but, with him, Malesherbes' relations were more affectionate, more constant, and also, inevitably, more tempestuous.

Their friendship began in the year 1750 when Malesherbes was appointed to head the Librairie. At almost the same time, the Academy of Dijon offered a prize for the best essay on a rather provocative subject: "Has the Progress of the Sciences and the Arts tended to Corrupt or Improve Our Customs?" In the middle eighteenth century, as now, academies were eager to show that they were not behind the times and to provoke attention. In this particular instance the academicians were not disappointed; Jean Jacques Rousseau submitted a reply. He maintained that progress had increased corruption and that the arts and sciences had encouraged lies, curiosity, and superstition. They were also responsible, he wrote, for the growth of luxury which had subsequently divided society unequally into the idle and the poor. The expression of such an opinion in an age when the leading philosophes had made almost a religion of the doctrine of progress created a sensation.

A second discourse presented to the same academy in 1755 gave Rousseau another opportunity to call attention to himself. The subject proposed was "On the Origin and Bases of Inequality among Men." In this thesis Rousseau took up the theme of the primitive state of humanity. He portrayed primitive man as free, solitary, animated with that pity which, he declared, is innate to everyone, living without wars or quarrels or rivalries until the first sin came, the fall—which was the introduction of private property with all its attendant evils.

This second discourse created an even greater stir than the first. It not only provided Rousseau with his principal theme but it opened the eyes of many. It showed them to what lengths the cult of nature and the prevalent fashion of idealizing the remote past might lead them. It also aroused the ire of the philosophers, some of whom loved comfort and enjoyed ease and competences. An attack ensued, which was led by Voltaire.

It was this controversy that first brought Rousseau to Malesherbes' attention. Everyone was talking of the reports of this latest performance. Few had seen the discourse, for it was not yet available, but there was a great demand for copies of the work which was in the process of publication in Holland. Marc Michel Rey, Rousseau's publisher in Amsterdam, wrote Malesherbes for permission to send copies into France and forwarded to him a sample. Malesherbes read it and was struck by the courage and daring of the author. He replied at once to Rey and granted his request. He even gave him the name of the best French dealer to handle the book. It appears that the enthusiasm of the director carried him too far. He loved anecdotes and novelties, and here was a new thing to hand. He read it aloud to his friends and spread its contents all over Paris; so much so that Rousseau felt constrained to protest that Malesherbes was passing his copy around Paris before the good people of Geneva, for whom it was written, had had a chance to see it. He begged Malesherbes to restrain himself: "And you, sir, who have never harmed a soul, you would surely regret having done injury to *un ami des gens be bien* who makes it a duty to honor you." Malesherbes was pleased by this gracefully worded request, agreed to keep quiet, and even returned to Rousseau the copy that he had. In due time, the discourse was put on sale in Paris.

A second controversy with the philosophes brought the two men closer together. After his second success at Dijon Rousseau had returned to Geneva. In order to become a citizen he had resumed his membership in the Protestant fold. At this time Voltaire, who was in Switzerland, was trying to introduce the theater into Geneva. This was, of course, contrary to the laws of the followers of Calvin. In an effort to support the plan of Voltaire, D'Alembert wrote for the Encyclopedia an article on Geneva in which he expressed the pious hope that the city would open a theater and so improve its taste. Rousseau, ever eager to attack Voltaire, took up the cudgels at once and published his *Lettre à d'Alembert sur les spectacles*. In this essay he attacked the theater and accused it of debasing public morals. He sent a copy to Malesherbes, who was amused by it and passed it on to D'Alembert. Malesherbes wished to have it distributed in France, and a very willing D'Alembert wrote him: "If you think it apropos to make me the censor, I give you my approbation in advance." Under date of July, 1758, he wrote again to the director: "I have read the work of M. Rousseau against me. It gave me much pleasure, and I do not doubt but that it will give the public as much enjoyment as it has me." Turgot read it, and Sallay, one of Malesherbes' inspectors, wrote: "You have read it yourself, and I therefore shall not advise you. . . . Like Don Quixote, he has seen giants where there were only windmills. Most of his ideas are well thought out and clearly and agreeably expressed. This makes us forgive him for the small number of remarks that are silly and childish." It was exactly this agreeable style of Rousseau's that made such an impression on Malesherbes and that first attracted the director to him. By 1758 Rousseau's reputation as a writer was established in France and the friendship between the two was known to the world of letters.

Although frequently in disagreement with him, Malesherbes recognized Rousseau's genius, admired his daring, and frequently took his part before the other philosophes whom he was continually antagonizing. Above all else, he was touched by his poverty. To relieve it he procured for him the offer of a post on the *Journal des savants*. This would have brought Rousseau a stipend of about eight hundred francs a year. To the chagrin of his protector, Jean Jacques declined.

Malesherbes often found him a very difficult protégé who needed almost incessant encouragement. In 1760, Rousseau, in one of his moods, wrote that he wished to abandon writing. In haste Malesherbes protested against such an intention: "Neither your health, nor the other reasons that you aver seem to me to be sufficient motives for your decision to renounce a literary career. It seems to me that literature should never be dishonored by the weaknesses of those who cultivate it, and in this time when a number of men abuse their talents, it would be a double misfortune if the clamor of a few should close the mouths of those who have only breathed out virtue and humanity." He concluded by urging him to continue the new work on which he had embarked. This was *La Nouvelle Héloïse*.

It is rather indicative of the plight of the book trade during the eighteenth century that this book and Rousseau's two other principal works were not printed in France. So great was the opposition of the Dévôts and so strong the dislike of a number of the philosophes that Malesherbes was unable to obtain this grace for his friend. In spite of this failure, however, Malesherbes, more than any other person, was responsible for facilitating the appearance of *La Nouvelle Héloïse* in 1760. But it was a long, hard struggle, a struggle caused in part by Rousseau himself.

Malesherbes had read a part of the manuscript and he liked it. He personally arranged for the proof sheets to come to him from Rey in Amsterdam. As Director of the Librairie, Malesherbes had the franking privilege, and by having the package addressed to himself he was able to relieve the fortunate author of considerable expense. But it

was always hard for Rousseau to believe that he was fortunate, and when these pages were slow in coming Rousseau wrote his printer bewailing his fate and attributing
the delays to Malesherbes, who, he said, had them but was
holding them up. When he was not making this accusation, he was expressing fears of piracy. And he was not
comforted when Malesherbes told him that he could not
always prevent such a thing from happening. Writing of
this period at a later time, Rousseau commented: "I always
regarded Malesherbes as an honest man. Nothing ever occurred that made me doubt his integrity. But he was as
weak as he was honest, and sometimes he did a little harm
to people in whom he was interested in order to save them
from a greater disaster."

This qualifying statement probably refers to an episode
that occurred when Malesherbes, at Rousseau's request,
examined the text of *La Nouvelle Héloïse*. In order to secure its author against the possibility of royal displeasure,
Malesherbes demanded the deletion of one particular sentence in the text. At a certain point in the story, Julie, the
heroine, was made to remark: "A charcoal burner's wife
is more worthy than a King's mistress." Malesherbes feared
that the all-powerful and naturally sensitive Madame de
Pompadour would take umbrage at this remark. For caution's sake he required a change. But it was only after re-
peated discussions and displays of temper that the change
was made. At last Rousseau yielded and wrote penitently to
his publisher: "I am touched and confused by the details
which he [Malesherbes] has been kind enough to consider, and it only remains for me to subscribe to all of his
orders and counsels."

During this same period a change had come in Rous-

seau's existence. He had broken with Madame d'Épinay
and stood in need of shelter and protection. The Duc and
Duchesse de Luxembourg had already shown an interest
in him, and it was at Malesherbes' suggestion that they offered Rousseau a retreat on their property at Montmorency. *La Nouvelle Héloïse* had been a great success, especially among sentimentally inclined ladies who wept over
the virtues of Julie whether she was wife, mother, or mistress. His benefactors now undertook the matter of Rousseau's latest project, *Émile, ou de l'éducation,* a pedagogi-
cal romance.

In certain ways, this book was one of the most profound
of Rousseau's efforts. It contained the whole of his philosophy. To many of his readers it was the most irritating.
Émile was supposed to represent Rousseau's conception of
the ideal man. Émile should be educated as a natural man,
not as a savant. He should be taught those things which
would assure the survival of his inherent goodness and his
happiness. Abstract philosophies, sciences, impractical
knowledge were useless and harmful; nature and experience alone should teach.

Rousseau's patrons did all in their power to help him.
Malesherbes personally went over the contract with his
publisher, for Rousseau was totally incapable of coping
with such matters. The Duchesse de Luxembourg was
persuaded to undertake the initial expenses. Then came
the time of publication. Philosophes were offended by his
scoffing at their profession and his protest against the introduction of reason into religious thought. And when
they came to the part where the Savoyard vicar professed
his belief in the sanctity of the Gospels, they declared that
Rousseau was now preparing to enter the cloister. On the

other hand, Jesuits and the Sorbonne were enraged by the words of this same vicar when he instructed Émile in religion: "I believe that all religions are good when they serve God properly. The essential religion is the religion of the heart." Nevertheless, there was a moment of success; young fops tried to imitate the manner of Émile and set themselves to work at carpentering while fashionable matrons began again to nurse their own infants instead of putting them out to nurse with peasants. Then the Sorbonne denounced the book and Parlement ordered it to be burned. Rousseau was actually threatened with arrest. He was hurried out of Paris by his friends and took refuge in Switzerland. He could not go to Geneva, for there both *Émile* and the *Contrat social* had been banned.

Malesherbes did not desert his friend. He did his utmost to help him, but this time he wished to defend Jean Jacques against himself. The first enthusiastic reception of *Émile* had been deceptive, and the condemnation which followed brought a disillusionment that Rousseau could not bear. He became more than ever solitary; in his opinion he was a martyr for the cause of honesty and humanity. He had always feared the Jesuits, but now he came to believe that they sought his destruction and that all mankind was deserting him. Even before his flight he had written Malesherbes a series of letters about himself. They reveal the intimate character of their relationship; some of them formed the basis for his *Confessions* which he wrote toward the close of his life. One of them shows very clearly his state of mind as he displayed it to his protector: "Finally, as long as my strength allowed it, in working for myself I have done what I could for society. If I have done little for society, I expected more from her and I think I

am quits with her. . . . If in my present state I could rest
and live from now on only for myself, I should do it without scruple. I shall at least rid myself, with all my power,
of public rumors. Should I live to be a hundred I would
not write a line more for the press. I shall not believe that
I am beginning once more to live until I shall have been
entirely forgotten. . . . I cannot hide from you, Monsieur,
that I have a violent aversion for states that dominate
others. I am even wrong in saying that I cannot hide it
from you, for I have no pain when I acknowledge it to
you, to you, born of illustrious blood, son of a Chancellor
of France, and First President of a sovereign court: yes,
Monsieur, to you who have done me a thousand favors
without knowing me, and to whom, in spite of my natural
gratitude, it does not hurt me to be obliged. I hate the
great, I hate their power, their hardness, their prejudices,
their smallnesses, and I should hate them even more if I
despised them less."

After his flight from France, Rousseau's condition became even more pitiful and his suspicion of persons increased. He was provoked to this attitude in part by the
violent attacks of Voltaire and the hostile attitude of the
Swiss pastors. Malesherbes wrote him constantly in a vain
effort to calm him. At length, in January, 1766, he was persuaded to go to England, and he settled there near where
Hume was living. But the delusion of persecution increased; now it was Hume and D'Alembert who were
maligning him. He wrote a long letter to Malesherbes
about it. Suddenly, in May, 1767, Malesherbes learned from
Turgot that Rousseau had fled to France. Hume wrote
to them both, urging them to find a retreat for Rousseau.
Turgot replied that Malesherbes would do all he could:

"You know the lively interest that he has always had in him, and to the natural enthusiasm with which this author inspires him there is as well a real sentiment that is based on his personal knowledge of the man. He believes that the wrongs which Rousseau has done you are to be explained by the violence of a character which is as impetuous as it is defiant."

In the early summer of 1767 Malesherbes located his friend and persuaded him to go into the provinces, to Savoy. There, he said, he would find consolation and peace in communing with nature and in doing as he had made Émile do—in working with his hands. Malesherbes also, alas, proposed to him his own sovereign remedy for all ills —the study of botany. For a little while Rousseau was docile. He even attempted to become a sort of assistant in research to his protector: "Unable to subsist without the help of my work, I never thought, in spite of the pleasure that it would give me, to offer you gratuitously the employment of my time. . . . Surely, sir, you, who in spite of all your knowledge never cease to increase it, will not deny me the pleasure of contributing to your amusements." Malesherbes accepted the offer. In the country and in Malesherbes' library in Paris Rousseau worked obediently for him and aided him in preparations for the *Herbier*. Soon, however, Jean Jacques' interest flagged. He wrote an angry letter to the master botanist, and their friendship cooled rapidly.

The experience with Rousseau was really more than an episode, for it left a profound mark on Malesherbes and influenced his career. It taught him, as nothing else could have done, the trend and temper of the eighteenth-century movement. At the same time it profoundly affected his future. The protection that he afforded Rousseau was taken even more seriously than the assistance that he had given the Encyclopedists. Although Malesherbes has left no mention of it and although he could not have approved of it, he was now regarded by many as a partisan of the *Contrat social*. The role of a liberal and benign protector was almost over, and now, more and more, he would be forced into becoming an active prophet of the fall of the ancien régime.

CHAPTER IV

MALESHERBES AND THE ANCIEN RÉGIME

MALESHERBES' first conflicts with the ancien régime had been as censor; in these he had acted
almost alone. His other struggle, as President of
the Cour des Aides, was carried on with an entire court behind him.

The tribunal which he headed was the court of final appeal for all civil and criminal matters concerning the *aides,
gabelles, tailles* and other forms of taxation; it alone had
the right of interpreting all ordinances that related to taxes.
For twenty-five years Malesherbes, as its president, opposed the disastrous system of taxation in France and urged
reform before it would be too late. Many of his suggestions
were subsequently followed by Turgot and by the National Assembly, which abolished completely practices for
which Richelieu and Colbert had been primarily responsible.

The principal features of this system were the wasteful
and arbitrary methods that the government used in determining the amount and rate of taxes and the farming
out of the indirect taxes to agents for collection. These
agents were entitled to retain a certain percentage of the
amounts collected to pay for their services while the "farmers-general" furnished the security for them. Against the
avidity of these farmers-general and against the careless
and thoughtless financial practices of the royal government the Cours des Aides throughout the country were in
frequent protest. In a certain sense, therefore, this branch

of Parlement became recognized as a protecting agency for the people of France, and it was primarily the experience in these tribunals that convinced some of the magistrates and the people whose interests they claimed to represent that some sort of reform must be made.

Nevertheless, the parlementaires were not spontaneous humanitarians. In the course of two centuries they had risen to great power, and upon very modest beginnings they had built an imposing structure of pretensions. Royal decrees had to be registered by these courts, and, on such occasions, the magistrates had the right to present remonstrances and even to refuse to register the edicts unless the King or his appointed representative were present.

As early as 1586, De Harlay, a presiding officer of the court, had addressed these words to the King: "There are two kinds of law, Sire: one is composed of the ordinances of the King which may change according to the times and necessities; and the other includes ordinances of the realm. These last are inviolable, and among them is one, the most holy, which our kings have always observed—never to publish a law or ordinance which has not been verified by this company."

Upon these basic privileges the courts of Parlement had constructed a claim to be the permanent custodians and guardians of the fundamental laws of France. There was not, they asserted, a single phase of life and action over which some one of the courts had not some control. Furthermore, by the opening of the eighteenth century, their members were wealthy and enjoyed considerable social distinction. In 1704 Louis XIV had admitted the magistrates of the higher courts to the rank of nobility, and now within this new class there had developed a series of

family "dynasties." There were the Pasquiers, the D'Ormessons, the Molés, as well as the Lamoignons. They possessed large estates, and, like Malesherbes, many of their
sons had married into important financial houses. Among
them there was now as great a pride and class conscious-
ness as existed among the older nobility.

Throughout the early part of the reign of Louis XV
there had been frequent challenges of royal power by this
class. The parlements of Franche-Comté, Dijon, Toulouse,
and Brittany had often threatened the central government
and its councils. They had impeded the carrying-out of
policies and even resorted to strike methods by adjourning
and refusing to hold their courts until their desires had
been granted. "There is but one free body extant, the Parlement, which represents the downtrodden people of
France." Assertions to this effect were frequently heard in
their courts. Reform and protest had become their almost
constant cries; as one of their number put it, "Many of us
were willing to go as far as the line of Revolution, but no
one of us would ever have crossed it." They were not, as
yet, adherents of the idea of revolution, but, in their efforts
to maintain their own rights and to keep the people on
their side, they played an important part in sowing the
seeds of discord in France. Long before the crisis of 1789,
Parlement, in all its branches, had laid down many of the
principles of the Revolution. Louis XV, then, was not mistaken when, in one of his wiser moments, he declared that,
for a full century, an *esprit frondeur* had animated most of
the noblesse de robe in France.

It was with such a tradition and with such a class psychology behind him that Malesherbes, in 1750, made his
debut as First President of the Cour des Aides. And his ex-

perience as magistrate taught him by practice what the
contact with eighteenth-century philosophy had proposed
to him in theory. The first severe lesson came six years
after his appointment. It was concerned with the inevitable matter of an increase in taxes, necessitated by the re-
sumption of war.

The conflict between France and England was resumed
in 1756, when Frederick II of Prussia renewed his war
with Maria Theresa of Austria. In the first of these wars,
which lasted from 1740 to 1748, France had sided with
Prussia principally because of the tradition of Bourbon-
Hapsburg rivalry, and because England had taken the part
of the Austrian Empress. For France and England the vi-
tal scene of the conflict had been in the colonies. Frenchmen, in general, were like Voltaire; they did not appreci-
ate the value of their overseas possessions. But Louis XV
and his ministers had realized how necessary they were to
the welfare and prosperity of the mother country. In India
and in America, during this first struggle, French weakness had been demonstrated, and the French government
had welcomed an excuse for peace when, in 1748, Frederick II brought to a conclusion his quarrel with Maria
Theresa. The interval that followed the peace witnessed in
Europe a diplomatic revolution and in France strenuous
but unintelligent preparations for another colonial duel
with England. Thanks to the Austrian Minister, Kaunitz,
France lost temporarily her dislike of Austria, while England shifted to the side of Prussia. In May, 1756, the Seven
Years' War broke out. This time the British made no secret of the fact that French competition in the matter of
colonies was to be brought to an end.

Louis XV and Choiseul were thoroughly aware of the

critical nature of this conflict. In a vain effort to patch up French military and naval power they proposed to add to the emergency taxes that had already been decreed during the last war and that were still in force. On July 7, 1756, the King and his council issued three decrees, one of which established a tax of a twentieth net on trade.

This tax aroused the ire of the bourgeoisie. Following the usual procedure, the edict was sent to the Cour des Aides for registration. But that tribunal, led by Malesherbes, invoked its ancient privilege and drew up a formidable document: *Très humbles et très respectueuses Remontrances que présentent au Roi, notre très honoré et souverain seigneur, les gens tenant la Cour des Aides.* It was dated September 14, 1756.

This manifesto was known to have been written by Malesherbes, and, once it had been published, the president became the hero of the hour. He was acclaimed as a defender of the people; delegation after delegation of merchants paid him visits of felicitation. He was even elected to the Académie des Inscriptions et Belles Lettres for this bit of prose.

As prose, the Remonstrances was nothing extraordinary. Malesherbes did not have the style of a Voltaire; he was an indifferent and rather verbose, heavy writer. There was no sparkle or facility of phrase; there was little grace to his sentences. But the content of the Remonstrances atoned for what was lacking in brilliance and eloquence. It was a courageous and merciless attack on the government for its foolish and unfair policies of taxation. Had these charges been heeded, the reign of Louis XV might have been a happier one and the rule of his successor might have lasted longer.

Malesherbes struck at the very heart of taxation abuses in France; he declared that one of the principal reasons for the financial distress and uncertainty in the country was the prevailing idea of the "perpetual character of an emergency tax." He demanded that, in the future, when special taxes were decreed, their temporary character should be stated and guaranteed. But the recommendations in the Remonstrances went further than that; they urged taxation for all classes of people in the country:

A tax which falls on each and every one of your subjects and which is proportionate to the wealth and size of each family would, no doubt, be the fairest arrangement. But a tax becomes unbearable when it is applied on the basis of hasty calculations, carelessly made a long time ago, and not in accord with existing facts and with justice. . . . A tax, we repeat, should be proportionate to the revenue of the taxpayer and should be applied to his benefit. But these new ordinances affect only men of business, and they are to carry all the burden. They already do so. That is the situation, Sire, to which the artisans and merchants of your realm are reduced, these citizens so indispensable to the State, who work as efficaciously in peace as in war to make your empire the most flourishing one on earth and to increase your wealth and power. It is entirely on this class that these imposts fall, imposts which we are not afraid to call odious. Their abolition we ask. . . . Among your other subjects, Sire, there are those who live on the patrimony of their fathers, and they use it up every bit every year without augmenting or diminishing the national wealth. These persons have never been included as taxpayers in your decrees. There are also others [the farmers-general] who have increased their fortunes and even amassed considerable wealth in the collection of your rightful dues; it seems to us that these gentlemen also should be assessed.

This protest virtually demanded as early as 1756 the abolition of the regime of privilege as far as exemption from taxes was concerned.

When the nature of Malesherbes' address became known, there was consternation among the Court, Church, and higher nobility, who feared for their purses and their privileges. At Versailles the rumor was current that the President of the Cour des Aides was trying to foment another Fronde and again, as in 1648, to lay siege to the King and his council. On September 22, Louis XV sent the Comte de Clermont, prince of the blood, to an extraordinary session of the Cour des Aides. He was accompanied by troops under the command of Maréchal de Bercheney. There, before the assembled magistrates, Clermont read the edicts and in the name of his royal master commanded that they be registered. The court, however, was determined to make its opinion felt, and Malesherbes replied to Clermont with a warning of the danger of arousing public sentiment. Then the court announced that it would proceed to registration. But debate continued. A few days later, the Duc de Chartres visited the tribunal and transmitted the King's order that the magistrates be silent and that all discussion of the edicts be stopped. The magistrates yielded, but not before Malesherbes had addressed himself to the prince: "Monsieur, you are about to perform, in the King's name, the most important act that pertains to his absolute authority. You should know that these magistrates upon whom you are imposing silence have only raised their voices in order to carry to the King the complaints of the people whom they represent. . . . I would remind you that your ancestor, Henry IV, once remarked about the same sort of taxes: 'These are illegal measures, for they derive only from force and violence.' We are not afraid to tell you, Monsieur, that hope will only revive in Frenchmen's hearts when they behold princes of the blood assuming the noble role of intercessors to the Sovereign for the cause of the nation."

At Versailles the reaction to these remarks was one of hostility mingled with amusement. "Usurper," "pompous Malesherbes," "the little dictator," he was called. Pompous he was and, at times, self-righteous. Dictatorial he would always be. There was a shade of truth, too, in the charge of usurpation. The Cour des Aides was not a legislative body by law or tradition, nor was it officially representative of the people. Neither Malesherbes nor his court, however, had been desirous of fomenting rebellion. All that they had intended to do was to lay before the King their criticism and their fears. This they had done, and then they had submitted to the royal order for the registration of the laws. But, at the same time, they had exposed themselves to the implication that some of their principles were exactly in line with the political doctrines of the philosophes. From the time of this episode, Malesherbes and the Cour des Aides were regarded by many of the King's Court and by the Church as Encyclopedists.

For a while there were no more Remonstrances. But Malesherbes seized every opportunity to bring his ideas to the attention of Louis XV. He appears to have bombarded the King with letters. It is doubtful if many of them ever reached His Majesty. In 1761 he wrote him concerning the practices of royal agents in the provinces and of the farmers-general: "The despotism under which your subjects groan is not the direct authority which Your Majesty exercises nor the indirect authority held by those who have your confidence. Rather it is a power given not only to the intendants, but also to a multitude of little men, without names or titles, without direct commissions from yourself, without having even been named by those who could speak for their qualities. . . . In such hands a sword has been placed, and this sword is more redoubtable than the sword of justice. Upon the arbitrary favor of these persons hangs the fortune of the hard-working farmer, the industrious artisan, and even the indigent noble." At the close of this address to the King, Malesherbes mentioned another practice—the lettres de cachet, a theme which he would pursue to the limit at a later date.

In fact, it was at this very time that he began an investigation of the practice of sealed orders which sent so many, without trial, into solitary confinement. There had been an almost constant protest about the condition of the prisoners, and Malesherbes started to build up a large dossier of evidence which he would use at a later time. Sometimes, even, he was made the dupe of impostors like De la Maire, who, in 1760, told a lurid tale of suffering which Malesherbes believed, only to discover later that the whole story was without foundation.

As a magistrate and as leader of the Cour des Aides, Malesherbes had shown himself to be far more advanced than his father. Chancellor Lamoignon was easygoing and conservative. He was regarded as allied with the Jesuits, whose expulsion he delayed. He was no longer popular. Furthermore, he was rapidly losing his influence at Court. Unlike his rival, Maupeou, he refused to make frequent appearances there, and he would not waste his time flattering the favorite, Madame de Pompadour. By the Court he was regarded as "très bourgeois et de très-peu d'esprit." Sprung from a family of parlementaires, once he had become chancellor he was more of a man of the government and enemy of the Parlement than any chancellor France had had for some time. Frequently, too, there had been clashes between Lamoignon and his son, the First President of the Cour des Aides. As early as 1753 D'Argenson had prophesied the chancellor's fall. It came in October, 1768, when Lamoignon was sent off to his lands and Maupeou, his rival, became vice-chancellor.

Many believed that a similar fate was in store for Malesherbes. He himself thought that he was doomed and wrote to his cousin, Lepelletier: "I do not wish you to learn first from public talk that we are being deprived of our functions. . . . My father has been exiled to Malesherbes, and I know not what my own lot will be. I shall leave my duties with deep regret." The fate of Malesherbes was soon made known. He was not sent out of Paris, and he remained President of the Cour des Aides. All that Maupeou did was to deprive him of his position as Director of the Librairie and Imprimerie. This was a change that was desired by the new vice-chancellor, by the Court, and by the Church. In the future, it was hoped, the censorship would be more rigorous.

The naming of Maupeou as vice-chancellor—for Lamoignon for a time stubbornly refused to resign the title —marked the opening of a struggle to crystallize the development of the absolute monarchy in France. Maupeou came in as a reformer, but his reform would not be in the direction desired by the parlementaires. He sought to concentrate all power in the hands of the King and a few of the King's ministers, and to remove, if necessary, the bloc of the parlementaires that, with its privileges and pretensions, stood in the way. This class was the object of Maupeou's principal hatred; he feared its pride; he abominated its corruptions, for the magistrates were accustomed to receive gratuities; and he denied its claims. When he discovered that he could not control it, he determined to break it. In 1770, two years after the disgrace of Chancellor Lamoignon, the opportunity came.

Despised by some for the failure of the Seven Years' War and blamed by others because France was unable to meet her war debts, Choiseul was losing favor. At the moment he was being blamed particularly by Court and by King for his inability to cope with the Parlements.

Even toward the lesser court, the Cour des Aides, Choiseul had observed a policy which was too lenient to satisfy the conservatives. Often he had shown himself unable to control and reduce the number of Remonstrances which had become such an embarrassment to the King. On almost every occasion the Cour des Aides and its president had hastened to take the part of any provincial court or individual magistrate involved in a controversy of rights with the government. From 1763 there had been an almost steady succession of Remonstrances voted and published on behalf of the parlements of Brittany, Dijon, Varennes, Montauban, and other important centers. The tone of these protests had not been to the liking of the King and the Court, and it was the expectation of Louis XV that the appointment of Maupeou would put an end to controversy. The publicity given to these affaires had been a source of constant embarrassment to the monarchy, and Choiseul had been warned that he must pursue a more vigorous policy against what was regarded as the interference of the Parlements. His position became all the more difficult when a long-standing controversy between the government and the tribunals came again to the fore. It was known as the "Affaire de Bretagne," and it concerned the actions of the government's Commandant of Brittany, D'Aiguillon, and La Chalotais, Procureur-Général of the Parlement of Rennes.

In accordance with the traditions of his own class, La Chalotais had desired his son to succeed him in his office. D'Aiguillon believed the son to be unfit for the place and refused to grant the license. At once the Parlement of Rennes supported, of course, the Procureur-Général, and a great part of Brittany, where the spirit of particularism was especially strong, rallied to the cause. D'Aiguillon remained obdurate. In an effort to make him yield, the Parlement of Rennes adjourned and suspended the exercise of justice in Brittany. Whereupon La Chalotais was arrested by the commandant's orders. D'Aiguillon had never been popular; the Bretons disliked his methods and there had already been the usual arguments over taxes. La Chalotais, on the other hand, had not only the backing of the Parlement but also the sympathy of the philosophes and their supporters, for he had stood out for the expulsion of the Jesuits.

Within a short while, the French government found that it had a famous case on its hands and one that threatened to become a national issue. The Parlements of the other provinces had become interested. At length the Parlement of Rennes instituted proceedings against D'Aiguillon. Finally the King's minister was able to arrange that the case should be transferred from Brittany and tried before the Parlement of Paris. But the King soon discovered that there the sentiment was decidedly hostile to D'Aiguillon, and, at the suggestion of Maupeou, he issued an order enjoining silence on the Parlement and declaring that D'Aiguillon should be tried by his peers. This move did

not succeed in stifling the affair, for the courts of the provinces were now aroused and there were demonstrations
and disturbances which Choiseul was unable to check. On
September 3, 1770, Maupeou as chancellor had the minutes
of the Affaire de Bretagne transferred to his own office
and forbade the Parlement to discuss the case. But, on
September 6, when that body met for the last time before
its vacation, the magistrates set a date for the discussion of
Maupeou's order. The matter was to be resumed on December 3.

This action of the Parlement of Paris received the enthusiastic approval of the provincial magistrates, who took
occasion to assure the Paris tribunal of their support. The
Affaire de Bretagne had become a case of the magistrature
against the government, or, as the parlementaires put it,
"of the parlements and the people against the arbitrary action of the King's council."

In the meantime, the government became embroiled
with the Cour des Aides. It was believed that a war was
imminent between Spain and England and that France
would go in on the side of Spain. Already deep in war
debts, France was about to contract more of them. The
Cour des Aides indicated clearly that it would do nothing
about registering the new taxes which were brought to it
unless Maupeou resigned. This was one reason for the controversy. There was a second and more immediate cause—
the Affaire Monnerat.

Monnerat was a tradesman who had been suspected by
the intendants and the farmers-general of dealing in con-
traband tobacco. He had not been brought to trial before
the proper court but had been deprived of his liberty by a
lettre de cachet and lodged in the prison of Bicêtre. While

there, it was reported, he had been confined in a *cachot* where daylight never penetrated, given only bread and water, held fast by chains, and brutally treated. He remained in this plight for twenty months. Then he was released and informed that his had been a case of mistaken identity. At once, Monnerat protested his treatment to the Cour des Aides. The court investigated all the circumstances and began a suit against the official who had been responsible. The farmers-general immediately banded together to protect their colleague and protested vigorously against the court's action. Maupeou and Terray supported them. At Terray's insistence, the King canceled the case which was before the Cour des Aides and forbade it to pursue the matter further. This edict was followed by a second royal decree which commanded the Cour des Aides to desist from the practice of any criminal procedures in the future. Such an order, if observed, would have deprived Malesherbes and his colleagues of one of their most important functions. The court, Malesherbes wrote, would cease to be a sovereign body and would become purely an appendage of the Ministry of Finances.

This was exactly what Maupeou and the council desired, and they determined to take this occasion to break the power of this Court of Finances. To do this, Maupeou had to convince the King of its rebellious and disobedient character. Hastily the chancellor summoned Malesherbes and thirty members of the Cour des Aides to Compiègne to hear the King's commands. Maupeou did not believe that the magistrate would arrive in time, for the Dauphin was moving to Versailles and the usual conveyances had been commandeered for him and for his household. But Malesherbes perceived the trick. Nothing daunted, he hurried over Paris, picking up carriages and hacks here and there and borrowing them from his friends. *Monsieur le premier Président* and his thirty colleagues arrived at Compiègne exhausted and shaken from the hasty journey over a very bad road. But they were triumphant, for they were exactly on time. Maupeou was embarrassed; the King was not prepared to receive them; even his address had not been written. And the chancellor was not really eager for the magistrates to have the opportunity of gaining the royal ear. They waited three hours. In the end they never saw Louis XV.

Maupeou's effort to discredit the Cour des Aides had failed. At the conclusion of the episode, Malesherbes wrote Maupeou a letter warning him of the danger the monarchy would run if he persisted in directing it along such a course: "I know, Monseigneur, how dangerous it is for a First President of the Cour des Aides to express, in his own name, views on affairs which concern the King's authority. But, in the present situation, personal danger should not be a consideration. It is impossible for me to refrain from beginning my remarks with the statement that the sole reason for this situation is the fact that your own council desires it. . . . A day will most certainly come when you will repent having attempted such a violent stroke against a court which deserved to be treated far differently." He requested the chancellor to show the letter to the King and warned him that he intended to publish it. This threat, Malesherbes later asserted, prevented Maupeou from going any further for the moment.

Upon their return to Paris, the magistrates reiterated their protests in the usual form of Remonstrances. Now, it was no longer a question of taxation abuses and the equalization of imposts, but of human liberty, authority, and justice: "Your Majesty has declared that you wish to close a trial which has already been begun before the Cour des Aides; but you ignore the fact that this investigation has already revealed the existence of a conscious and planned system of despotism at the expense of the law . . ., which would substitute arbitrary acts for normal procedures. . . . The result is, Sire, that no citizen in your realm is assured of his liberty, for there is no one who is great enough to be secure from the hatred of a minister. . . . Your Majesty should be prepared, from this investigation, for revelations of the most flagrant abuses of his authority; these abuses impede not only the course of justice but even human liberty, which is the first of all laws."

Later, on April 11, 1771, when the final blow had come, Malesherbes wrote: "I was prepared since last year for all that would happen to me. . . . The chancellor wished to intimidate by example the Parlement with which he was then beginning to quarrel, or else he desired to try his strength against a less powerful company. Doubtless also, the several intendants of finances or the farmers-general themselves wished to seize this occasion to get rid of a company which has always been a redoubtable overseer. Today, when this object has been accomplished, I conclude that my letter was not even given to the King."

In the meanwhile, Maupeou and the Parlement of Paris were continuing their struggle. Soon Malesherbes and his associates would be called to the defense of their entire class.

On December 3, the Parlement of Paris reconvened. Maupeou went before it, and, speaking in the King's

name, he forbade it to use in the future such expressions
as "unité, indivisibilité ou classe de la magistrature." "By
using these terms," he said, "the magistrates claim to be an
exclusive and uniform body throughout the kingdom, and
an hereditary class." In subsequent instructions the chancellor defined the powers of the Parlement and reminded
its members of their limitations:

When the legislator [the King] wishes to manifest his desires, you
are his organ. His goodness allows you to exercise your knowledge
and to show him what you believe to be the truth.

There your function ends.

The King, in his wisdom, then weighs your observations; he
balances them against the motives that provoked his own action,
and, with his broader vision which embraces the whole monarchy,
he decides between the advantages and the inconveniences of the
law.

If he commands, then you owe him the most complete submission.

Although Maupeou was probably less well versed in the
law than the parlementaires whom he was attacking, he
saw straight to the core of the issue. In his eyes the whole
quarrel appeared to involve the question of the old monarchy or revolution.

His instructions aimed a blow at the political and social
prestige of the noblesse de robe. Its members should have
taken more heed of the danger which lay in wait for them.
Even on December 24, when Choiseul, who had been so
lenient with them, retired, and when Maupeou, D'Aiguillon, and Abbé Terray assumed the control of the King's
council, they remained obdurate. "At last," wrote a lady
of the Court, "Louis XV will actually reign, and his enemies will fall before him." There was little doubt to what

enemies the elegant lady referred; it was the expectation of many that now the magistrates would either submit or else be dismissed.

But submission was the last thing of which most members of the Parlement were thinking. The majority of them were determined to bring about the disgrace of Maupeou. And this disgrace they sought not so much for the nation as for themselves. There were bitter recriminations on both sides. By the magistrates Maupeou was held up as an example of the ambitious and corrupt statesman. Malesherbes remarked: "The Court is a country where you only keep your head up by evil and often criminal intrigue." To which Maupeou, who was stupid but honest, retorted by references to the childish prattle of *mon bavard ennemi*. Between the families of these two men there had already been bad blood. In 1750 Chancellor Lamoignon had received the office which Maupeou's father had coveted; but now Maupeou had more than outstripped Lamoignon and his progeny.

This hostility to the new minister, however, was not confined to the powerful clan of which Malesherbes was a member; practically all of the "dynasties" of the noblesse de robe stood against Maupeou. But their reasons were not the same. Some were fighting for their privileges, of which Maupeou, for reasons of state, was seeking to deprive them. Others like the D'Ormessons, the Lepelletiers, the D'Aguesseaus, and the Lamoignons were struggling as well for a national principle in which they honestly believed.

On January 3, 1771, the Parlement of Paris resumed its meetings. The court indicated that it would never recognize Maupeou's instructions of the preceding December.

On January 15, it again refused to accept the new order of things and adjourned. Four days later soldiers visited the homes of many of these magistrates with lettres de cachet: "Sir, I send you this letter to tell you that it is my intention that you resume at once the function of your office and fulfil the ordinary service which you owe to my subjects for the expedition of their business . . . and that you do this without interruption or discontinuance, and that . . . you remit to the bearer of this present letter, without tergiversation or deceit, *by simple declaration of yes or no,* signed in your own hand, your acquiescence to submit to my orders, understanding that I shall take your refusal to explain your actions and to sign as disobedience to my orders."

Most of the magistrates of the Parlement of Paris stood by their resolutions. On the following day these were exiled to their homes, and their offices were declared forfeited. Maupeou then instituted a part of his reform; hereafter justices should not receive gratuities, they should no longer own their posts and transmit them, and they were to be remunerated for their services by the Crown. From now on they were to function as justices in ordinary civil tribunals.

This action against the Parlement struck close to the Cour des Aides. In a special session that tribunal charged its president with the preparation of a protest on behalf of "these virtuous magistrates." On February 17, the Remonstrances were ready. In them Malesherbes on behalf of the Court defended the attitude of the exiled judges and denied that they had been seeking to instigate rebellion. Their existence, he declared, was necessary for the security and happiness of the people. "Now there is no resource, no protection for the people of France." He tried to show that the cause of the Parlement was the cause of the nation. The events of January 19 and 20 were proofs of a rapidly growing arbitrary and despotic power. Furthermore, the action which abolished the old courts was contrary to the law: "There are things, Sire, which even kings may not do. . . . Our silence would have made the nation accuse us of treason and cowardice. The rights of the nation are the only rights which we demand today. . . . The courts are today the only protectors of the weak and the unfortunate. For a long time there has been no Estates-General, and, in the greater part of the realm, there are no provincial Estates; and the other bodies, except the courts, have been reduced to a mute and passive obedience. No single person in the provinces would dare to expose himself to the vengeance of a commandant, of an agent of the council, or, even less, of a minister to Your Majesty. . . . Up to this day, at least, the demands of the courts took the place, although imperfectly, of the demands of the Estates; but now the last resource left to the people has been removed. Let the question be put to the nation, Sire, since it is only the nation that may be heard by Your Majesty."

This demand that now, since the Parlements were no more, the Estates-General should be reinstituted, placed Malesherbes, in the opinion of the Court, right in the front rank of the revolutionaries. It delighted the philosophes of course. After reading the Remonstrances, Abbé Morellet wrote to Condorcet: "I am now going to dress and go—where do you suppose? To Monsieur de Malesherbes. Since there are still in France men like him who combine great talents with great virtues, I am proud to be his friend, and I feel how glorious it is to be a Frenchman." Morellet, however, knew that Malesherbes was not a radical. In reality, the president was royalist to the core, but Louis XV no longer believed his protestations of faith in the monarchy and characterized him as *un encyclopédiste dangereux.*

Alarmed by this drastic proposal of the Cour des Aides, Maupeou saw no other way left but to bend it to his will or else to break it. The Register of the Cour des Aides carries this entry under date of February 18, 1771: "On Monday . . . the *Gens du Roi,* in accordance with an order of that date, went to Versailles. They were unable to see the King; the chancellor told them that he would see His Majesty on Tuesday and that he would advise them as to his intentions." Three futile visits to Versailles were made by the court, but none of them brought an audience with Louis XV. On March 9, the Cour des Aides met in formal session to consider their reply to the King's refusal to receive their communication. They instructed the president to protest against the new tribunals and voted a long series of statements concerning the recent actions of Maupeou and the council. Forbidding the court access to the throne indicated, they asserted, the project of overthrowing the constitution. They deplored the prohibition placed on publicity, an act which stifled the voice of the public. Again they affirmed the belief that they were the sole remaining representatives of the nation.

Nothing more was heard from Versailles until the morning of March 26, when Malesherbes and two officials of the Cour des Aides were summoned there by La Vrillière. On the following day they presented themselves at the house of Maupeou. "The chancellor, whom we found rather embarrassed, for he knew not how to begin the conversation, asked the first president if we had been cold on the way. The first president replied that he thought not, and added: 'But when shall we see the King? It is for that we have been summoned, and it appears that you are well aware of the fact.'" The chancellor was impatient to know when Malesherbes intended to inform the court what was going to happen once he had been apprised of it himself. To this Malesherbes, who had a very clear idea of what was in store for them, replied that he expected to tell some of the members informally upon his return to Paris that very evening. Maupeou, however, insisted that Malesherbes should call a formal meeting that night. He followed the first president to the house of La Vrillière. Once there, he raised the question a second time. Again Malesherbes refused to commit himself, and then added that he could not have a full meeting of the court until Quasimodo (the first Sunday after Easter) because some of the members had gone off to their homes to keep Holy Week. To this Maupeou replied: "You do not wish, then, to assemble the Chamber this evening? I believe that you are wrong."

Maupeou's plan appeared to have been to involve the court as soon as possible in a heated debate on its rights in which it could be charged with lese majesty. This would have served him as a convenient pretext for its suppression. Malesherbes saw through the scheme, and this explains his procrastination. Later he wrote that he had desired to give the Cour des Aides the longest possible lease on life. His enemies firmly believed that he had the hope of arousing public opinion to action.

It was on April 7, the day following Quasimodo, that

the final blow came, when Monsieur de Richelieu brought to the Cour des Aides the order for its suppression. A number of its branches were dissolved, and the new Parlement of Paris was to consist of the Grand Council and a few members of the Cour des Aides. The bloc of the magistrates had been broken; the course of the monarchy had been cleared, but it was cleared to lead to ruin.

On April 6, Malesherbes, who had already arrived at his country house, received a lettre de cachet confining him to his estate. He had expected the blow, and he was not alarmed. "All I can say about what concerns me is that, if the desire to ruin me has contributed to the misfortune of my company, it is all that the most injurious and most cruel vengeance could have imagined."

"My one consolation is the thought that the only steps by which I may have irritated the government are my letter of last year to the chancellor and the Remonstrances made by the court, either last year on the lettres de cachet and the Affaire de Bretagne or a little while ago on the affair of the Parlement. My letter to the Chancellor was necessary to prevent them from executing against the company what has just been done in 1771. And, as for our different Remonstrances, it seems to me that the public, by whom they are known, has judged that they appeared under circumstances in which the companies as well as private individuals should have sacrificed themselves for the good of the State."

As to his retirement, he accepted it easily, perhaps even gratefully. To an intimate friend, he wrote: "It is high time that I retired, for I feel that each day I am losing a bit more of my reputation as a philosophe."

CHAPTER V

THE Remonstrances of 1756, 1763, and 1771 reveal
the fact that, during this first period of his public
career, Malesherbes' social and political ideas had
developed rapidly. From the vague idealism of Fénelon,
with which he had begun, he was now fast approaching
the more definite line of thought expounded by the philosophes. But it may by no means be asserted that his political thought was molded by them alone.

Some writers have believed that Montesquieu exerted a
preponderant influence on Malesherbes. It is true that he
owned Montesquieu's works and knew them well. In 1775,
when he was received into the Academy, his address contained several references to Montesquieu. But very little of
the responsibility for Malesherbes' development may be
laid at that door. As a matter of fact, Malesherbes had frequently found himself in disagreement with Montesquieu's ideas.

In June, 1767, Malesherbes had written a critical commentary on two of Montesquieu's works—*The Grandeur
and Decadence of the Romans* and *The Spirit of the Laws.*
"If you ask me why I criticize so famous a man as Monsieur de Montesquieu, I will reply that I do so precisely
because he is famous. His name gave his errors a sort of
consecration, but truth merits more consideration than a
famous man himself." He did not deny the dignity and
worth of the philosopher's efforts, but he could not agree
with a number of his interpretations and proposals. Male-

sherbes protested that he had none of Montesquieu's veneration for Rome: "I hate the Romans because they created the unhappiness of the world; I despise them because they did not know how to be happy, because they preferred a false, foolish, and cruel glory to a solid and lasting one." He could not accept Montesquieu's ideas of government and laws, their origin and their character; Malesherbes abhorred all complicated systems, and he did not believe in the importance of environment and climate as determining the various forms of government and law in the world: "C'est parcequ'on a envie de se mêler de tout qu'il faut tant de lois différentes. Quand on ne veut que protéger les bons contre les méchants et assurer à chacun sa propriété, il n'est pas besoin de tant de lois et les lois nécessaires à ce but conviennent aux habitants de la terre." Montesquieu, he wrote, relied too much on worn, existing systems and thought too little of the new: "Monsieur de Montesquieu was cautious, as are all men of the law for whom novelty is always an object of terror; but for a man who is called upon to govern, novelty is neither good nor bad; he should believe as did the Marquis d'Argenson, who remarked that a really good government should be a perpetual novelty."

The principal influences affecting Malesherbes were of a more personal sort, his environment and his own character and habits. The traditions of his class, the esprit frondeur of the magistrature, and his own experiences as President of the Cour des Aides gave him every chance to observe and to examine the necessities of the time and the motives of those in power. But a more important factor was his own habit of study. Unlike his father, the ex-chancellor, Malesherbes was an independent thinker, and he had always been a close student of institutions. Like many of his contemporaries of the eighteenth century, he was profoundly interested in the question of their origins and primitive character, and he spent a great deal of time in personal investigation.

At the Château Tocqueville where many of his papers are to be found, there is a mass of notes in his own hand relating to the origin and early character of the French monarchy. From them it appears that Malesherbes had carried his investigations back into the more remote history of France; a great number of these fragments of small, square sheets of paper carry notes on the Crown and its practices from the times of Clovis and of Charlemagne. They continue down to the reign of Louis XIV. There are quantities of citations from historians of note of the seventeenth and early eighteenth centuries. There are extracts from law codes, capitularies, and commentaries as well as, later, quotations from Gibbon. Many of them are written in his more legible and youthful hand, others in his later and very difficult scribble; all of which indicate that this practice of study extended over a very long period of time, and these notes and extracts are very closely related to the principles which he asserted in the public documents that appeared over his signature.

Malesherbes' conception of kingship was clear and well defined. He believed in kingship by divine right, but, he asserted, divine right placed upon the monarch marked duties that were really limitations. "God," he wrote, "has only placed crowns on the heads of kings in order to assure their subjects of security, liberty of purpose, and the tranquil enjoyment of their rightful possessions." But that this monarchy should be a limited one, in the generally accepted sense of the term, he was not so sure: "Monarchy is nothing more than despotism itself, but it is moderated by a certain established order which it does not seek to overthrow, because it has no interest in so doing. . . . In Denmark, where the most absolute despotism is consecrated by law, the government is as moderate as in other countries where they speak of an intermediate power, subordinated and dependent." Laws exist to limit the power of monarchy, but they are natural laws. These laws are infractible and when they are violated by a monarch, even for good cause, there is no guarantee of security in the future. "When the principles of government are destroyed, the personal virtues of a king cannot guarantee the realm against a total subversion beyond the life of that king." The only safeguard for the welfare of the people, therefore, is for them to have a means of consulting the monarch and for the monarchy to be able to consult them. "For, after all," he writes, "the kingship was established by the people's wish." Like Fénelon, Boulainvilliers, and Montesquieu, Malesherbes believed that this was true of the earliest times and that down through the centuries, consultation of the king and the people had been a usual practice. He interpreted, in such a light, the concilium and other assemblies of the earlier monarchy. And he did not hesitate to apply these same interpretations to the monarchy of his own day: "Let the question be put to the nation, Sire; the incorruptible witness of its representatives will tell you, at least, if the cause which we are defending is not the cause of all the people by whose will you reign and for whom you reign." These words he would again address to the King on the eve of the Revolution.

There had always been, he wrote, a body representing the nation. Once it had been known as a National Assembly; then it became the Estates-General. Finally, since 1614 the Estates-General had not been called, and Malesherbes believed that the courts of Parlement had taken their place. This much was the opinion of many of his fellow magistrates, but Malesherbes did not stop there. He was willing to acknowledge that, while Parlement had substituted as best it could for the Estates, the Estates themselves, if recalled, would be superior to Parlement and sovereign with the King. From the time when he first saw the existence of Parlement threatened, he became one of the most persistent advocates of a renewal of the Estates-General, or, failing that, the establishment of provincial Estates throughout France. In one or the other he beheld the sole means for unifying and reforming the country and for bringing under control the "little people," by which he meant that vast army of petty officials who were making such an abuse of power. In the action of the nation through the King and a national assembly he saw the only remedy for the unequal burden of taxation and the practice of lettres de cachet, which violated human liberty and interfered with the authority of the courts of law.

From this, however, it should not be inferred that Malesherbes was the advocate of the domination of any particular class—bourgeoisie, nobility, or clergy. Nothing that he ever did or said would lead one to believe that he would have approved of the first victory of the bourgeoisie which came with the Revolution. Like many of the nobles and most of the greater philosophes, he had only scorn for the bourgeois and his interests. He completely failed to realize the coming importance of the middle class to the nation. "A population which is based on commerce and manufacture has only a precarious and temporary foundation." Nor did he favor wealth: "Great fortunes are good for nothing; they do not make for happiness. Whoever has studied men and beheld the ennui of the rich is convinced of this truth." In his opinion, a happy and successful society was not to be found in any system of class; not among nobles, who, he wrote, were never a bond between monarch and people, but a bond by which the monarch bound the people; nor yet a privileged class, like the parlementaires. His ideal was a nation whole and unified under the King and bound together by equality. This state of things, he argued, it would be very easy to establish: all that was necessary was the abolition of privilege. "It is not necessary to establish a rigorous equality; all that should be done is to remove the great inequalities. . . . It is absurd that all men are not equal in the eyes of the law when they are all equal in the eyes of nature. It is the law to protect equality there. All privileges are based on prejudices or on injustices. Those who, by chance, have been recompensed by privileges hold them as the result of a shortsighted view which fails to take into consideration the unhappiness of others. There is no privilege accorded to one person which has not done harm to another. It is unjust to favor one part of the nation at the expense of the rest. As to privileges of long standing, they are held on titles which are almost always vicious in their origin. In the opinion of the philosophe, you may never prescribe against the interests of the people."

This was the point to which Malesherbes' political philosophy had attained when the Cour des Aides was closed and he himself, by Maupeou's lettre de cachet, was confined to his estate near Pithiviers. Like Montesquieu, his starting point was a legal one, but he had not gone to the

point of setting other than moderate limitations on royal
power.

HE had arrived at Malesherbes shaken and exhausted, but
he soon regained his calm. Political questions were for a
time abandoned. Paris was forgotten, and his entire attention was given to his family, the company of his daughter,
and the affairs of his estate. When friends reproached him
for his apparent lack of interest in the events of the capital, he replied, "What would you? Like Leibnitz, I love to
see my gardens grow and watch the plants whose seeds I
have sown."

This period of exile was marked by the greatest activity
in agricultural experiments and in botanical studies. During the busy days in Paris even, he had not abandoned his
hobby. At that time the popularity of science and nature
study was at its peak. The Jardin des Plantes, which had
been so carefully developed by Buffon, was the scene of
gatherings of fashionable ladies, courtly bishops, and gal-
lant gentlemen who learned a little but not too much
botany. Malesherbes himself had no use for these *fripons,*
as he called them. He was to be seen there apart from them
and alone, a more serious visitor. He had also, at odd moments, continued his examination of Buffon's *Histoire
naturelle.* Once the exile had begun he set to work on his
own *Herbier* in earnest. It was to go into forty volumes!

At the same time he was occupied in transforming the
gardens on his estate. "He planted in his gardens at Malesherbes a quantity of shrubs and exotic plants; these he

EXILE AND RECALL

had even acclimated, and he had multiplied them to such an extent that, in strolling through his woods, one might fancy oneself transported into distant regions where acacias, palms, and the trees of Palestine grow. High rocks, magnificent waterfalls, and majestic pines added still more to the illusion, forming a singularly picturesque situation, and a display of enchanting scenery." The estate of Malesherbes became famous and was the show place of the countryside. But its owner made it, as well, almost a school for the study of agriculture.

In other parts of France local academies of science and agricultural societies were springing up like mushrooms. Ever since 1761 the government had been encouraging these methods of stimulating agriculture in the rural districts. Malesherbes was determined that the Orléanais should not fall behind the other provinces and he now took hold of the group that had already been formed in that section. Its members were neighboring landlords and the more important cultivateurs. At frequent intervals they met at his house and heard reports of new discoveries or viewed the experiments which Malesherbes himself was making. Inevitably, these discussions about farming methods and means for the improvement of agriculture led the society to the question of agricultural policies and the government. Gradually, here at Malesherbes, as in other parts of France, the agricultural society became "philosophic." Possibly in the Orléanais group this development was more pronounced because of the friendship that already existed between Malesherbes and one of the leading physiocrats of the day.

Farther west in France, Anne Robert Jacques Turgot, now intendant in the Limousin, was making an experi-

ment that soon attracted the attention both of government
and landlords. By his policy of removing age-worn restrictions, the survivals of feudal practice, Turgot was transforming his province from a poor district into a flourishing country. Turgot's experiments and economic policy
now became a part of the discussions of the Société de
l'Agriculture de l'Orléanais. Physiocratic idealism began to
have its effect, and the condition of the small farmer became a matter of grave concern to the enlightened country
gentlemen and landowners who gathered occasionally at
Malesherbes. And the owner of the estate himself became
the advocate of a greater freedom for the tenantry. His
lands assumed a new significance in his eyes.

Into this pastoral, almost idyllic existence came, in May,
1774, a rude intrusion. News arrived that Louis XV was
dead.

The realization that the reign had ended shocked
France, but, within a few days, consternation gave way to
another sentiment; Frenchmen believed that an era of enlightened rule had come. Although he was young and in-
experienced, it was common belief that the new King
would not be such a ruler as his predecessor had been.
There would be no more Court scandals; Madame du
Barry had fled. Louis XVI was known to have no favorites
except his Queen whom he feared and idolized. He was
serious and well intentioned. Unlike the late King, he had
given evidence of a determination to learn the art of governing. The triumvirate of Maupeou, D'Aiguillon, and
Terray was over. A happy coincidence had prevented
Maupeou from seeing his new monarch. He and his two
companions had been constantly at the deathbed of Louis

XV, and, since the King had died of smallpox, there was fear of contagion.

Strong advice had come to the young couple concerning the choice of a ministry. Maria Theresa had written in haste from Vienna to her daughter: "*Point* de premier Ministre." Maupeou was more unpopular than ever, and Louis XVI desired to make it evident that there would be a change in attitude and in policy. He selected, therefore, the most agreeable man at hand, Count Maurepas, an experienced courtier, of good manners and pleasing appearance. Maurepas, too, at the beginning had good intentions, but he was not a serious statesman. To Maurepas the King joined Vergennes, who took over the Department of Foreign Affairs, and Turgot, the much-discussed intendant at Limoges, who was made Minister of the Marine. At the same time the King announced that certain levies, usually connected with an accession to the throne, would not be required. May, 1774, was a month of rejoicing, so much so that Parisians practically ignored the desolate cortège that arrived one day carrying the plague-stricken body of Louis XV to the tomb at St. Denis where it would rest undisturbed for so short a time.

As one reads the letters and memoirs of this spring of 1774, which show the happy expectations of Frenchmen, it is hard to believe that this season marked the beginning and not the end of a tragedy. D'Alembert wrote paeans in praise of the young King to Frederick II of Prussia. It was believed that relief and good will would come at last. This new King was not burning for expensive wars to retrieve the loss of distant colonies. Voltaire, even, began to think about preparations for a return to Paris, where, four years later, he would enjoy so strenuous a triumph as to kill him. And the dispersed parlementaires saw, in the reign that was beginning, a promise of their own restoration. As if to cap the climax, on August 24, it was announced that Turgot, Minister of the Marine, had been made controller-general of the realm.

When he assumed the control of French finances, Turgot's plans were already formed. His experience as intendant of Limoges had convinced him that his program was a sound one. He believed that "the State exists only to protect the rights of all by assuming the fulfilment of mutual duties." To enforce such an idea he felt that a benevolent despotism, like that of Russia or Prussia, was necessary. His ideas on financial policy were clear: "No bankruptcy, no increase in taxes, no loans." And to make this possible he envisaged a system of economy by retrenchment in government expenses and by the abolition, or at least the reform, of the farmers-general. For the relief of the people he intended to reduce the local tariffs, to establish the complete freedom of the grain trade, and to abolish the corvée on roads that was required by the government. This was his initial plan. It included most of the principles of the physiocrats and met some of the demands of the philosophical writers. Almost from the moment of its formation the new council was known as the "Philosophical Ministry," a name which was not entirely to the taste of Maurepas.

There were other evidences of change beyond the immediate province of Turgot's department. Hardly had Maupeou retired than an agitation was begun for the restoration of the Parlement. There were some who questioned the wisdom of such a move; among them, at first, was Turgot. The demand from the people, however, was very great, and there were demonstrations in the streets of Paris in favor of the magistrates' return. At this time Maurepas was eager to please everyone, and he became spokesman for the movement before the King. It was agreed that it should be made clear to the magistrates that if they should be restored they could not again challenge royal authority. As time went on Turgot's own mind changed, and he became inclined to favor their recall; he believed that one tribunal, the Cour des Aides, under Malesherbes, would be of great assistance to him. At the Court there were two parties of opinion, the party of the Patriots and the party of the Dévôts. The Dévôts desired things to remain as they had been, but the Patriots, led by the Duc d'Orléans and the Prince de Condé, were not untouched by the current liberal teachings, and it was among them particularly that the agitation was begun. Once it was under way, many of the philosophes who previously had held back from the Parlements gave the idea their hearty approval and supplied the necessary publicity by means of pamphlets. On November 12, the Parlements were restored and were instructed by the King in person as to the limits of their powers.

Two days before this date, Malesherbes, in his retreat, received an order to appear on the twelfth in the place where the Cour des Aides had formerly sat. On the appointed day, the King's brother, the young Count d'Artois, attended by a great company, reëstablished the tribunal and recognized Malesherbes as first president. There was a great display of emotion. The newspapers outdid themselves in their descriptions of justices falling into the arms of princes.

Following the reading of the royal edict, Malesherbes replied to the prince. He began by praising the young monarch for having consulted the wishes of the nation concerning the choice of his ministers. Then he launched into a long prophecy, too optimistic, alas, of the reign that was beginning. There were references to the preceding regime and the late unpleasantness with the Parlement, but they were veiled and were only brought in, one may be sure, as lessons for the future. "If ever there should arise again such turbulent spirits as often exist in troublesome times, if ever they should dare to utter those pernicious maxims that power is never sufficiently respected unless terror walks before it; that the administration of a country should be a mystery hidden from the people by reason that subjects have a perpetual tendency to disobedience and, when they supplicate, desire only to rebel; that authority has an interest in maintaining those in power and those who abuse it; that the King's most faithful friends are objects of hatred to the people, then, Monseigneur, it will be enough for our King to recall what he has beheld in this, the earliest hour of his reign. And you, sir, who have witnessed this scene and who sit beside his throne will, we trust, remind him incessantly with what solicitude, sincerity, and overflowing heart the whole nation has received her young monarch. This France expects from you and from all who, like yourself, are dear to the King and interested in his prosperity." On December 28, Malesherbes and the Cour des Aides set out in solemn state from the Sainte-Chapelle for Versailles to thank the King for their restoration.

Beneath all this display of eloquence and of good will on these two occasions there was one very serious implica-

tion; by the utterances of its president, the Cour des Aides,
like the other tribunals, indicated its firm intention to admonish the King and to keep him informed of the opinion
of the country. Even deeper down, though not so evident
at the time, was the fact of an alliance between the controller-general and the Cour des Aides, an alliance which
created, for a time, such a union between the administration and this court as had not been known for years. The
firm friendship between Malesherbes and Turgot was its
basis. Every early step in the way of reform that Turgot
made was reënforced, even, at times, predicated by the
Cour des Aides. Formally and informally, Malesherbes instructed the King concerning his most difficult problem—
finances. Frequently he participated in private discussions
with the King and his controller. When Turgot put forward the abolition of restrictions and of revenue on grain,
Malesherbes supported him in the face of the protests of
the *gens d'affaires*. When he recommended the abandonment of government corvées and the curtailing of expenditures, the President of the Cour des Aides put in a strong
word of approval. In these days, Turgot had the confidence of many of the élite who had espoused the cause of
reform. Walpole writes that everyone he knew and met at
the house of Madame du Deffand and in the other salons
he frequented applauded the Turgot-Malesherbes combi-
nation.

But, after the first few months of his ministry had passed,
Turgot stood in greater need of support and encouragement. From the first he had had the financiers against
him. Another category of the opposition was the party of
the Dévôts; Turgot did not go to Mass. He had also advised the King against using the traditional ceremony of

coronation. The fact that he had done so in the hope of using the money that would be saved to relieve the country was not taken into consideration. Gradually members of the Parlement, too, began to turn against him; he wished too much to come from the King and too little to be done by them. In 1775 all these elements began to grumble against the policy of the controller-general and to claim that the freeing of the grain trade was working harm. The harvest of 1775 had been bad. The price of bread had risen. Nobles and English buyers of French grain were stirring up the people against these policies. Later in the spring there came riots and the march of protesting families—the army of Jean Farine—to Versailles.

Malesherbes stood by his friend, but now it was only with difficulty that he brought the Cour des Aides into line. They recommended finally what he desired: a careful revision of royal finances and expenditures and a reduction of taxes, particularly the gabelle, the tax on salt, which forced the people into smuggling. They also requested the distribution of taxes among all classes in France and the dismissal of insolent and corrupt farmers-general.

Such outspoken language caused consternation among those who held sinecures. Even that amusing and delightful Frédéric de Maurepas felt that these latest Remonstrances were a bit too precipitate. He remarked to Malesherbes that there was no hurry: "We have a whole reign in which to reform abuses." But Malesherbes was impatient and stood out for immediate action. This was necessary, indeed, if Turgot was to succeed.

It had been the custom for years to print and distribute

the Remonstrances. But these protests of May, 1775, were so strong that the King and Maurepas feared to have them published. To the dismay of Louis XVI and his minister, the Remonstrances, however, appeared and soon were in circulation. For this act Malesherbes may have been responsible; at any rate, the blame was placed upon him, and he bore the relentless hatred of the more conservative members of the King's circle from that day forth. At once, the Cour des Aides was commanded to decree the suppression and confiscation of the copies. The magistrates obeyed.

But, in the end, this episode of May, 1775, was not a defeat. The Remonstrances had given the first public expression to the entire policy of Turgot. Nevertheless, it was believed for a moment that the alliance of Turgot and Malesherbes had been weakened. The Register of the Cour des Aides for the séance of July 8, 1775, carries this note: "This is the last day on which Monsieur Delamoignon Malesherbes, First President, will attend the Cour des Aides." On July 12, his resignation was announced. As early as July 9, Madame du Deffand was writing to Walpole the news that Malesherbes was expected to replace the Duc de la Vrillière as Minister of the Royal Household. On July 12, the Cour des Aides broke an age-long precedent and went in a body to Malesherbes' residence to congratulate him on his expected appointment. The visit was a bit premature, and now that he was no longer one of their number and likely to become associated with the Court, of course they did not forget to admonish him: "We believe that the infectious air which you are about to breathe will not contaminate such a spirit as yours, and the entire nation, con-

fident in a magistrate who has defended its rights with
such magnanimity and unselfishness, remains persuaded
that truth will ever be the same in your mouth."

These prophecies and felicitations were bitter to Malesherbes. He was an *homme de la loi,* he protested; he was
not an administrator. The courts of Parlement were his
stamping ground. He could not easily assume the airs and
graces of the courtier. Many believed, and they were right,
that he could not take on their insincerities.

In a fever of doubt he fled Paris and went to his estate
to compose his mind and to find courage to renounce the
honor that was within his grasp. But at Malesherbes he
found no peace. In the course of one night three couriers
brought him urgent appeals from Paris. The last packet of
letters had its effect. The first letter was from Turgot, in
which the controller-general stated that, unless Malesherbes joined him in the King's council, the cause of reform was lost. The other note, in the same packet, came
from Louis XVI: "Monsieur Turgot has informed me of
your repugnance for the office that I propose to you; I still
believe that your love for the public good should conquer
your dislike for the position. You cannot know the pleasure that you will give me by accepting my offer, even for
a little while if not for longer. I believe that it is absolutely
necessary for the welfare of the State."

CHAPTER VI

IN THE KING'S SERVICE—
FAILURE

"YOU were indeed right, sir," wrote D'Alembert to
Frederick II of Prussia, "your praises of our young
monarch are justified. He has made an excellent
choice of ministers, and he has just named as successor to
the Duc de la Vrillière, who, to the great relief of all, is
at last going, the man who is probably the most respected
person in the entire nation, Malesherbes, who will work
with Turgot for order and economy. There is great alarm
in the camp des fripons. Between Turgot and Malesherbes
the future of these persons will be unhappy."

These sentiments were echoed by the comments of Mademoiselle de l'Espinasse and many others. Madame du
Deffand addressed the following remark to Horace Walpole: "Our government is now filled with philosophes.
Here is the reign of virtue and disinterestedness, of love
for the public good and liberty." Even Count Mercy-Argenteau, Austrian Ambassador to France, wrote Maria
Theresa telling her of his own approval and of the general
satisfaction of the country. The press, too, was delighted,
and its pages were covered with bad verse in which they
welcomed the now completed ministry:

> De Ministres quel choix heureux
> Et quel présage pour la France!
> Malesherbes tient la balance;
> Turgot préside à la finance;
> Saint-Germain combattra pour eux.
> Et Maurepas, par sa prudence,
> Rendra leurs travaux fructueux.

For a brief moment Malesherbes was the most discussed man in France. Contemporaries assert that his appointment created even more of a sensation than Turgot's nomination had aroused several months previously. The newly-appointed minister was at the height of his fame; his popularity at this time was greater than at any other period of his life. His Remonstrances of the preceding May had marked the climax of his efforts as President of the Cour des Aides; and now more was expected of him, more, unfortunately, than he would be able to fulfil. His elevation was generally regarded as the triumph of the philosophes. In addition, his reputation had only recently been increased by another honor; he had been elected to the Academy. The official reason for his selection was his ability as an orator. All other competitors had withdrawn when he had been persuaded to propose his name.

The press of the day described his reception into the fold of the Immortals as one of the most brilliant spectacles ever seen: "Tout Paris était là et jamais il n'y avait eu autant de femmes."

When he arose to make the customary address, the atmosphere of the amphitheater was tense. Would Malesherbes confine himself to a purely conventional eulogy of his friend and predecessor, Dupré de Saint-Maur? Or would he finish with that as briefly as possible and proceed to develop further the principles which he had expressed in his Remonstrances? Discourses at the Academy often had been turned to political purposes. Those, and there were many of them, who anticipated a sensation were not disappointed.

He began with a brilliant eulogy of public opinion, which he described as the sovereign tribunal of all tribunals on earth. This remark must have made some of his hearers wince. Then he turned to a consideration of the development of an enlightened public opinion in France. It was during the reign of Louis XIV, he declared, that the Academy had reached its full importance and had become an invaluable means for the enlightenment of the nation. He launched into a panegyric of that age which had witnessed such a renaissance of learning. "This was a glorious epoch, when science made powerful strides, when intelligence drove out that barbarous prejudice which had condemned our ancestors to ignorance. The name and purpose of every science were recognized, and savants of all classes received the consideration which was their due." To the surprise of his audience, when he reached the period of Louis XV, he ignored its political aspects and continued his narrative of the succeeding stages of enlightenment. Louis XV, he said, was interested in science and had about him a group of savants. He encouraged their efforts and paved the way for a continuance of the revival. "Today the secrets of the arts have been revealed or are about to be revealed. We have found that for which man sought during the past ages—artists capable of writing and readers capable of understanding them. . . . The study of nature, even, is no longer cold contemplation; it moves the soul with aspirations as powerful as those of the epic." It was, too, during this period of Louis XV, he declared, that the era of freedom began to dawn. This was due to several important men, among them his predecessor, Dupré de Saint-Maur. "The time has passed when a government seeks to bury in secret archives where they are soon forgotten such precious treasures." The republic of letters has come. "And now each citizen works for the state and each statesman is enlightened by his fellow citizens. In this way the various professions, characters, and talents are all drawn by a common tendency toward a sole purpose, and that purpose is the happiness of men. . . . And now human reason has perfected itself; humanity seems to be reborn in the hearts of men and has begun to drive out the relics of barbarism."

He concluded on a note of pleading to the new King and the new government of which he and others hoped so much. "Happy is the monarch who is destined to give laws to a nation from which all the prejudices contrary to human happiness seem to be disappearing." It is the duty of King and princes, he ended, to grant an increase of this freedom and to apply it to the realm of letters as well as to laws and government. "Princes should devote their efforts to introducing literature into their countries; but in a nation already instructed, where science and talents are revered, the most precious of all possessions, for men of letters, is the liberty of giving free rein to their genius."

It was Malesherbes the philosopher, the optimist, and the believer in Turgot's reforms, who had spoken, and not Malesherbes, homme de la loi. This was his last plea on behalf of the principles for which he had so steadily fought while he was Director of the Librairie.

In spite of his fame and these recent honors, perhaps because of them, the admission of Malesherbes into the King's council had been a difficult thing to accomplish. Time and again Louis XVI had refused to listen to Maurepas' suggestion. At one time, the King had tried to end the matter by remarking: "I know, indeed, that he is the one whom everyone wishes, but he does not suit me. I have told you so before now." The King was fearful of Malesherbes because of his policy when he had been Director of the Librairie, and his address at the Academy had increased his reputation as a liberal. However, Louis XVI bore him no personal resentment.

The real source of the opposition lay in another quarter; it was to be found in the Court and with the Queen. The fact that Malesherbes disapproved of privilege was well known, and his attitude particularly toward the Court nobility made the greater nobles inevitably hostile to him. Aside from the fact that they did not fit into his program for equality, he believed that they were an economic hindrance to the country. "The rights of the nobles interfere with commerce and place a heavy burden on the greater part of the nation." But he opposed them not only for their feudal rights and their sinecures but also because they held great landed estates, while he favored the redistribution of lands. "The best legislation imaginable," he had written, "is that which would multiply as much as possible the number of small farmers. This is something which our modern economists do not realize." Such theories, if put into operation, would have struck hard at the very basis of the resources of the nobles. They had come to fear Malesherbes. And, in this attitude, the Queen was on their side. As usual, Marie Antoinette had her own candidate, D'Énnery, beloved of the clergy and friend of Choiseul. His presence in the council would have embarrassed Turgot. The King was well intentioned and easily influenced; the Queen and her circle, therefore, feared the effects of having Malesherbes and Turgot in the same council, while with D'Énnery there would have been little danger of innovations and experiments.

Patiently and skilfully, Maurepas worked, and finally,

after the middle of July, he had maneuvered the King into granting Turgot's reiterated demands for his friend. Once he had yielded the point, Louis XVI received his new Minister of the Royal Household with marked cordiality; not so, however, the Queen.

As late as August the Austrian Ambassador reported to Kaunitz: "The nomination of Malesherbes went directly against the wishes of the Queen. When he was first presented to her she received him very coldly. Shortly she changed her tactics and, on the next occasion, she gave him a cordial greeting." Nevertheless, to Marie Antoinette, Malesherbes was always an enigma. She did not understand his bonhomie, and she disliked his passion for philosophy.

The truth is that, of the two friends, Malesherbes was the less fitted for the life of the Court. Turgot was austere and honest but sharp and inscrutable; Malesherbes, on the other hand, was honesty, gaiety, and good will itself, a rather corpulent hail-fellow-well-met. Unlike Turgot, in his dealings with people he was direct and simple. Furthermore, his behavior scandalized the Court. He had little use for their conventions. During one of the early days at Versailles, he met La Martinière, first surgeon to the King. A group of courtiers was present. The two men wore the drab costume of their professions. La Martinière approached the Minister of the Royal Household, poked him in his very prominent paunch, and shouted, "Bonjour, pater." Malesherbes riposted with a lunge at the abdomen of the first surgeon and a "Bonjour, frater."

Although given to dignity, Malesherbes was not elegant, and he was often far from being perfectly groomed. Ministers were required by the protocol to abandon their mag-

istrates' costume and replace it by "bourse et épée." Malesherbes persisted in wearing his former costume.

From the moment of his arrival he felt embarrassed at
Court, and he was confused by the intrigues and insincerities about him. Long before his nomination, he had
been aware of the character of the Court with which he
would now be in almost daily contact. In 1767 he had written: "All the virtues of the Court may be reduced to an exterior of confidence and friendliness which deceives no
one in general and very many people in particular." His
new situation was not unlike the one in which he had
found himself when he was censor; and he had little confidence that he would ever be able to accomplish all his
plans. He had accepted his mission with a fervent belief
in reform, and his program was the only thing which interested him. His intimates relate that he was in a constant
state of agitation about the uncertainty of things. "They
will be the ruin of us," he would exclaim, *"ces petits messieurs* who, after having been in the morning the first to
favor a change of things, declaim, at their suppers where
they form their opinions, against a new order. At first
their mood seems to be only the momentary sulkiness of
spoiled children; but wait, you shall see." Early in October,
1775, Walpole dined with Malesherbes at the house of
Madame de Villegagnon, and was much impressed with
his honesty, straightforwardness, and common sense. But
a few days later he wrote to Countess Ossory that the simple fashions of the Minister of the Royal Household were
beginning to amuse the Court. He added: "Designing men
who have no weapon against good men but ridicule already employ it to make a trifling nation laugh at its benefactors; and if it is the fashion to laugh, the laws of fash-

ion will be executed in preference to those of common
sense."

At the very outset, then, Malesherbes, like Turgot, met
with a quiet and determined hostility at Court, from the
clergy, and from the more important financial magnates
who disapproved entirely of the physiocratic theories of
the controller-general and his friend.

THE Minister of the King's Household had supervision not
only over the Royal Purse and expenditures; he also had
the direction of the affairs of the clergy and of the Protestants, the control of all pensions and appointments at
Court, and the administration of Paris and the most important parts of the *pays d'état,* which comprised the more
recently acquired provinces such as Burgundy and Pro-
vence. The Court, the town, and the Church were, then,
in Malesherbes' hands. In view of the courage and determination that he had shown in the Cour des Aides, one
might have expected him to have rejoiced at the prospect
of such power. Instead, there is every evidence of a real
perplexity and unhappiness: "Turgot's position is frightful,
but my own is hardly less dangerous. With all the best intentions that I have for doing good, how much evil may
be done in my name, and I may never know of it." Nevertheless, once installed, he set himself instantly to putting
his department in order.

One of his duties as administrator of Paris was the supervision of the prisons and of the lettres de cachet. The lettres de cachet had been used frequently by his predecessor,

La Vrillière. Actually the practice had not been employed as often as some have believed, but, for a full century, there had been constant talk and protest about it. In his earlier Remonstrances, Malesherbes had inveighed against this privilege which enabled anyone of prominence to obtain, upon presentation of a complaint, a sealed order from the Crown condemning an enemy to immediate imprisonment or exile. His first thought was to investigate the prisons where these unfortunates were usually incarcerated. He visited Bicêtre and found terrible conditions there. On September 9 he inspected the Bastille. He was horrified by what he beheld and became convinced that much that the philosophes had written and popular rumor had made of these cachots was true. He examined the cases of some of those whose pleas had never been heard, and obtained the release of a few. One man refused liberty, saying that he could not sacrifice his free lodging unless he was given enough to live on outside. This was done; he obtained both his freedom and fifteen hundred livres provided, it is said, from Malesherbes' own purse.

Malesherbes returned from these expeditions appalled by the misery, injustice, and disease that he had found. He talked about it everywhere. He met Walpole a second time and told him of his experiences. Walpole writes that Malesherbes' account made the tears run down his cheeks. Convinced that he now knew the truth, the minister decided to appeal to the King and to beg him to go and see for himself. Maurepas advised against this step and remarked: "The King must not go. If he sees the prisons, there will be no more prisoners." But Maurepas' objections did not deter him, and he laid the matter before Louis XVI. The King was moved by his report and instructed

his minister to continue his investigations and to liberate
any who had been unjustly confined or who had been imprisoned for too long a period. "As for me," Louis XVI
said, "I will not visit a single prison. Continue your good
work, Monsieur de Malesherbes, but do it without ostenta-
tion." Malesherbes proceeded cautiously, but Court rumor
exaggerated his activities. "On ne voit que des prisonniers
élargis," a courtier remarked.

The liberation of a few unfortunates and the improvement of prison conditions were merely temporary abate-
ments of the evil. At the bottom of the whole matter
lay the practice of the lettres de cachet. Obviously these
were being abused, but the fact remains that they were essential props of royal power. This last point Malesherbes
failed to consider; for many years he had had the abuse of
the system before his eyes. During the preceding reign, the
Cour des Aides had protested against the sealed orders.
Malesherbes had openly condemned the practice and described it as a form "of personal vengeance in which no
one is great enough to escape the hatred of a minister, or
little enough not to merit that of a clerk." Again, in the
famous Remonstrances of 1775 he had denounced it as a
mark of despotism. Now, while he was a minister, came
the chance to act, and Malesherbes set himself to work
upon a memorandum which recommended a change in
the administration of the lettres de cachet: "Your Majesty
would be horrified at the picture that one could give him
of all these innocent persons who, at the command of a
powerful person or a favorite, have been plunged into a
place of crime. You would be appalled by these unfortunates whose punishment, perhaps merited, has been ag-
gravated and prolonged with a harshness which has no

limit. There are many, even, who have languished in a long captivity or died simply because they have been forgotten. Since the goodness and wisdom of a monarch cannot prevent him from being the pretext for such an injustice, how much more should this privilege which exposes him to charges for which he is not really responsible weigh on his heart. For these orders that bear your name are fabricated far from you, and when they are presented to you they appear cloaked with specious reasons and charges. Since you have not the force to prevent the exercise of this fatal power, there is only one resource left to you, and that is to have the courage to abdicate it."

Had it been possible, Malesherbes would have preferred to abandon the practice entirely. Maurepas and others showed him that there were times when speedy imprisonment was necessary. Accordingly, in this case as in the matter of censorship, he had to compromise. He proposed to the King the formation of a special tribunal of magistrates to be selected from among the members of the Cour des Aides. These men should have charge of all cases calling for summary justice or lettres de cachet. And, furthermore, the powers of this tribunal should be so defined as to prevent their abuse and a too lengthy detention of any individual whose case fell within the jurisdiction of these special magistrates.

In making such recommendations, the author of the memorandum was not working only for humanity's sake but for the King's cause as well. His letters indicate clearly that, by the close of the year 1775, Malesherbes had become seriously concerned about the state of mind of the country and the security of the monarchy. There is an echo of this anxiety in the words that he wrote to the King: "Your greatest concern is that your authority should be not only respected but also blessed and cherished, and that it should be no longer the occasion for murmurings and complaints. In rendering it more dear, you will also make it more secure. The justice of kings and the love of peoples are the most solid foundations of authority."

To Malesherbes' great encouragement Louis XVI took kindly to the suggestions. The King foresaw the opposition that would come if the lettres de cachet were abandoned, and he was also aware of the real necessity for their use under certain conditions. But he permitted his minister to institute a tribunal, extra-legal, an advisory council in theory but a tribunal in fact. To this body all requests for the issue of lettres de cachet should be referred. Although never legalized, this commission exercised its functions throughout the remaining months of the Turgot ministry.

Nevertheless, Malesherbes was not satisfied. He had persisted in the hope that the practice would be abandoned entirely or, at least, that the reform would be given the authority of duly established law. "I never would have believed," he wrote to Boissy d'Anglas, "that the support of the King is the feeblest of all supports that a reforming minister can have. We had the King on our side, . . . but the Court was against us, and courtiers are now more powerful than kings."

Among the other duties of the Minister of the King's Household was the supervision of religious affairs. Both Turgot and Malesherbes had had the question of religious liberty at heart for some time. In 1754 Turgot had published a tract with the monumental title, "The Conciliator, or Letters of an ecclesiastic to a magistrate on the right of citizens to enjoy civil tolerance for their religious opinions, on the right of the clergy to resist with the whole power of the Church errors of which they disapprove, and on the duty of the prince in both cases." Malesherbes, too, had been investigating the problem. He had held many conversations with representatives of the reformed religion in France and was in frequent correspondence with Rabaut Saint-Étienne, one of their leaders at Nîmes. He felt that he knew the Protestants thoroughly.

In fact, he had made quite a study of their religion and their ethics. He was by no means convinced that they were wrong, nor, for that matter, was he certain that the established faith was right. "We should be very sure," he wrote, "that it is not our own religion which is wrong. I fail to see why we always imagine that it is right." It is, indeed, not unlikely that, like many others of his century, he felt that religion was a matter of public utility and a matter for the individual, and, therefore, he believed in tolerance.

In 1775 the situation of the followers of the reformed religion was becoming critical again. Since it was only the Church that performed marriages, Protestant unions were not recorded and, therefore, were not regarded as valid. Registration of births occurred only when the Church administered baptism, so the legal existence of Protestants was not recognized. It was claimed by the Protestants as well that often their children were forced to assume the Catholic faith. At this time, moreover, churchmen, stung into action by the campaign which was being waged by Voltaire and the other philosophes for the Protestants, began a campaign of their own for the extirpation of all heresies. Turgot, therefore, as soon as he was in office, presented Louis XVI with a memorandum on the justice and necessity of religious toleration. Thus far the King appeared to have ignored it, but in July, 1775, many regarded the appointment of Malesherbes as an answer.

It is true that no sooner was Malesherbes in the council than he and Turgot concerted upon a plan to force the adoption of a policy of toleration in France. It is also true that in this effort they received the hearty support of the philosophes and that the campaign of the philosophes contributed, in great part, to the difficulties of the two ministers.

Malesherbes' first move was to forbid bishops to bring pressure to bear upon Protestant children. Along with Turgot he advocated the establishment of lay instruction and an arrangement that would recognize the validity of Protestant marriages. He also seconded Turgot's plan for a reduction of the financial privileges of the clergy. But the inauguration of even such slight reforms and the intimation of others that were to come fed the antagonism of the party of Dévôts and the bishops. In vain in July, 1775, Turgot met the clergy in their assembly. All that he could get them to concede was a gift of money to the government and the acceptance of a sanitary measure that forbade the general practice of burial in city churches.

In the meantime, the philosophers took hope from the interest that the two ministers were manifesting and from the apparent acquiescence of the King. Unwisely, they renewed their campaign, and with a vengeance. Voltaire published the *Diatribe à l'auteur des Éphémérides,* in which he attacked not only the clergy but the Parlements, and protested against the amount of property held by the religious orders. D'Holbach, in his *Théologie portative,* set forth in alarming array the arguments against the divinity of Christ. In reply, the bishops warned the King against

the "monstrous atheism which has become the preponderant opinion in the country." They confused the recommendations of the ministers with the arguments of D'Holbach. They were unable to distinguish between tolerance
and hostility. At length the bishops appealed to the Parlement, and there they found support; a number of books
and tracts were condemned, and the King was solemnly
admonished to command his ministers to cease their efforts and to postpone the pursuit of liberties for the reformed religion.

This campaign aroused enemies in a new quarter. The
clergy had always been hostile to Turgot and suspicious
of Malesherbes, but now they had brought Malesherbes'
former associates, the parlementaires, into the quarrel. The
regime of intolerance established by the law of Louis XIV
continued for eleven more years. "Nearly all legislators,"
commented Malesherbes, "make the mistake of believing
that a law which is good in one century is also good in another."

Seeing Turgot beset by an increasing array of enemies,
Malesherbes proposed an expedient which had been in
his mind for a long time. When President of the Cour des
Aides in 1775 he had recommended to Louis XVI the calling of a National Assembly. "The unanimous desire of the
nation," he had said, "is to obtain the convocation of the
Estates-General or, at least, provincial Estates." This was
the suggestion that he now made to Turgot. He had investigated the matter all over again. He had written to
persons of note in the provinces and, from their replies, believed that an appeal to the nation would justify Turgot
and turn the tide that seemed to be going against them.
But Turgot rejected the plan. The controller-general still

clung to his opinion that the reform should be brought about by means of an enlightened despotism. He expected everything to be done by royal authority, and he felt that it would be dangerous if royal authority made the concession of an appeal to the people. This refusal was, perhaps, one of his greatest mistakes.

The more popular Turgot became with the philosophes and the people, the greater became the number of his enemies at Court, in the Parlement, and among men of finance. The crisis was reached in January, 1776, when Turgot presented to the King six edicts for registration by the Parlement. From that time on, the controller-general had to fight desperately to survive the animosity that met him at every turn.

The January edicts would eventually have transformed the whole appearance of French society. One edict suppressed the royal corvée on roads. It provided that this service which formerly had been required of the peasants should be replaced by a tax to be levied on all landed proprietors, who were the parties most interested in the good condition of the roads, and also on the King for his own domains. The money collected in this fashion was to be assigned to a Bureau of Bridges and Highways which would undertake the maintenance of all the roads in France. Such an arrangement would relieve the peasant of the interruption of his own work whenever the corvée was demanded. But the most significant aspect of the proposal was the fact that, if passed, the law would mark the beginning of the equalization of taxes; the nobles, clergy, parlementaires, and wealthiest of the bourgeoisie were the greatest landowners in France, and most of them were exempt from land taxes. At almost the same time as the appearance of Turgot's proposal came a shower of pamphlets from the greater and lesser philosophes. The tracts praised Turgot's plan, of course, but they treated it as marking merely a beginning in the general trend toward the abolition of all feudal rights. This interpretation put the privileged classes on their guard and increased their suspicion of Turgot's measures.

Along with the edict on the corvée there was a law relating to the corporations and masterships. Ancient custom had provided that no one could enter a craft or trade or own a shop unless he had become a member of the métier, gone through its grades of apprentice and valet, presented an adequate masterpiece, and paid a fee for his mastership. Later the fees had become almost prohibitive, and, in many crafts, the corporations had developed into family monopolies. These developments severely restricted the admission and promotion of new members, and, not infrequently, they interfered with the progress and growth of the craft. Turgot's law declared that any skilled worker, even a foreigner, might exercise the craft that he desired after registering a declaration of intention with the properly designated police official. This liberty, however, was not to be extended to crafts that had been officially established by the royal government.

In proposing such a reform, the controller-general was not acting entirely from humanitarian motives. There was also a practical bent to his plan; he desired to improve industrial methods, and he was particularly anxious to make it possible for English artisans with their newer methods to enter France. In other words, he was working toward an acceleration of the industrial revolution in the country.

To this proposal the monopolists were naturally antagonistic, while there were many of the artisans who did not even wait for the edicts to be registered. In Paris a number of them left their masters at once and tried to set up their own shops. There were riots and disturbances when they were informed that they had not yet the right to establish their own businesses. In some instances it was necessary to resort to force to quell the disorders. The blame for this violence fell on Turgot, even though he had used all the power at his disposal to put down the uprisings and to quiet the impatience of the artisans who thought that the day of their freedom had come.

While Turgot was occupied with the struggle over public reforms he left to Malesherbes and to Saint-Germain the regulation of economy in their departments. Saint-Germain accomplished the necessary reforms in the Military Household with little difficulty. But Malesherbes encountered insurmountable obstacles when it came to establishing economies in the Royal Household. For these changes involved the privileges, comforts, and pleasures of the great courtiers, many of whom were now completely hostile to the ministry. Malesherbes proposed to reduce the royal living expenses and to abandon the *arrêts de surséances* by which nobles were frequently granted long extensions for the payment of their debts. For these changes the King was willing, even eager. But when it came to curtailing the *Grand commun,* the service of the royal kitchens, which fed the hosts of people at the Court, the trouble began. Malesherbes himself was loath to continue the struggle unless he could persuade the King to undertake the reforms personally. In an effort to reveal to Louis XVI the reasonable character of his plan he drew up for him a *Mémoire sur la Maison du Roi;* "You came to the

throne at a time when economy was the general desire of
the realm, which was exhausted by the extravagances of
your predecessors. . . . The people of France and of Europe recognized in you two virtues which are the opposites
of extravagance—justice and a profound love of order and
system. I dare tell you, Sire, that it is only the people of
the Court who feel that your dignity depends upon all this
magnificence, and that a simple exterior, the retrenchment
of luxury and superficial grandeur, will increase the veneration which you will inspire in your subjects and in
foreigners. . . . But so drastic an alteration of things cannot be the work of a minister alone. The King himself
must consent to each one of the sacrifices with a full understanding of the reasons therefor."

It was the abandonment of the grand tradition of Louis
XIV and the lavish display—the *Fastes de Versailles*—that
Malesherbes was seeking. Turgot had shown him the balance sheet which would not balance, and Malesherbes was
thoroughly alive to the economic danger in which the government stood. At the same time, when he drew up the
Mémoire, he knew that it was a plea to which there would
probably be no satisfactory response. That is why he inserted at its conclusion the following reference to himself:
"Your Majesty thought it best to call me to the ministry
and give me charge of his Household. You know with
what reluctance I assumed my duties, and you will recall
that it was only an order from yourself that compelled me.
You were good enough to state that my service would last
for only a little while. Without entering today into all the
reasons for my retirement, I wish to say that one of the
principal motives is the absolute necessity for the reform
that I have proposed and the very little aptitude that I feel

for a task which has no relation whatever to the calling
that I have followed all my life."

Discouraged because of his three failures, with the lettres de cachet, with toleration of the reformed religion,
and with enforcing economies at Court, Malesherbes had
decided to withdraw. But, as he indicated, there were also
other reasons for this resolution; he was aware that the
attitude of the Court to him had changed. In the beginning he had been accepted at Versailles as a pleasant,
amusing, and rather original person, but now he was
feared and, in some quarters, despised. In the *Correspondance metra* one reads: "Already Malesherbes is no longer
a zealous patriot, a victim for the public good; he is now
an *encyclopédiste, un homme à système,* who is ignorant
of the affairs of the world." Kindly, generous, and sincere,
he had not the robust virtue of a fighter; chatty, he could
not always be talking of serious things. There is a pa-
thetic phrase that occurs in one of his talks with Baron de
Moleville; Malesherbes tells of trying to distract the King
with his anecdotes, and adds: "Mes bavardages le faisaient
rire quelquefois." But when affairs became serious and
pressing he wearied of having to repeat so frequently his
arguments to the King, and Louis XVI, too, became tired
of his sermons. Also, by February, 1776, Malesherbes had
again lost favor with the Queen. Marie Antoinette had
been annoyed by the proposed reforms in her household,
and she became rebellious when pensions to her intimates
were refused. Malesherbes failed utterly to understand her.
Once she had given him her confidence, he believed that
it would last for all time. And when, toward the end, he
was so unwise as to speak to her unfavorably about a favorite, Monsieur de Guines, her reply was to turn from

him and to find appointments and promotions in rank for those against whom he had spoken. He had spoken out of turn and concerning an affair which was not within his province. There were some who believed that Maurepas, desirous of embroiling Malesherbes with the Queen and her circle, had persuaded him to make this fatal mistake. "He has lost public esteem, and has not been successful with the Queen; we are practically certain that he will retire very shortly," Madame du Deffand recorded.

But, more than all else, it was the situation of Turgot after the New Year that influenced Malesherbes in his decision to resign. He had come into the ministry primarily to serve his friend and to uphold his principles. But when the conferences between the King and Turgot became less frequent, and when Maurepas turned against him, Malesherbes felt that he stood in the way and that he was released from his promise of service. He had specified carefully that he had only accepted his post for a little while. In his own opinion he had failed, and to continue the effort would be only to spread greater antagonism. With his hope went his courage. And failure came.

In March, 1776, to the perplexity of the King and to the delight of the opposition, Parlement turned against the Ministry of Reform. In despair, Louis XVI summoned the magistrates to Versailles for a *lit de justice*. There Séguier led the attack against the January edicts and declared that Turgot had set the whole country in a state of panic. There was truth in this statement, except for the fact that Turgot was not solely responsible for the condition of the country. Skilfully Séguier admitted the existence of abuses and then raised the cry: "Reform but not destruction!" The King listened attentively to the protest against registration of

the proposed laws and closed the session with the words:
"You have heard the edicts which my love for my subjects has dictated. It is my intention that you conform to
them."

For the last time Louis XVI sustained Turgot. But this
time it would not be a victory. Parlement reiterated its Remonstrances; Marie Antoinette and the Court continued in
their antagonism to Turgot and Malesherbes. The country was in a ferment of economic uncertainty and excite-
ment. Philosophes and other well-wishers of reform were
in despair. In April, Malesherbes retired, and the disgrace
of Turgot was only a matter of a month's distance.

"In short, Sir," wrote Horace Walpole, "I think the re-
sistance of the Parliament to the adorable reformation of
Messrs. Turgot and Malesherbes is more phlegmatically
scandalous than the wildest tyranny of despotism. . . .
Now that they have fallen, the Choiseuls and Louvois will
replace the 'Patriot Philosophers'; then we shall be forced
to see the wisdom of the Stamp Act and of persisting in
taxing America."

It was, indeed, the eve of the Revolution.

CHAPTER VII

PRELIMINARIES OF THE
REVOLUTION

FOLLOWING his retirement, Malesherbes set out on a walking tour which took him into the more remote parts of his own country. He visited the Alps, the Pyrenees, and Brittany, not as a *petit seigneur* or as an ex-Minister of State, but as a simple Monsieur Guillaume, *herboriste,* who was passionately devoted to botany. He spent his days studying the countryside and gathering information which he could use in his *Herbier*. He avoided the large towns where he might have been recognized. The nights were spent at small inns, where he talked with the people and learned from them their customs, their ideas, and their needs. He delighted in associating with simple folk and in studying their ways: "I have not met with anyone from any class of the people from whom I did not learn something that I had not known," he remarked.

Sometimes his efforts to remain incognito were not successful. In the Pyrenees, one evening, he met an officer of Dragoons. The officer remarked that there had been only one good minister at Louis' Court and that was Monsieur de Malesherbes. Malesherbes replied that he believed the reasons for such a reputation were specious. The argument became rather heated, and the officer concluded: *"Monsieur le naturaliste,* you do not like Malesherbes; I am astonished, for I thought you were a good man." To which Malesherbes, much amused, replied: "I have personal reasons for not wishing to flatter him." At this point a servant appeared and addressed Malesherbes by name. The officer saluted and said, "Monsieur, the enigma which perplexed me has been explained; you are the only man who could speak evil of Malesherbes."

Later, during his rambles in Switzerland, Malesherbes encountered a gentleman named Wittenbach who introduced himself as a minister. "And I," replied Malesherbes, "I am an ex-minister." In the course of their conversation Wittenbach offered Malesherbes a parish in his canton. Malesherbes declined the offer, without disclosing who he was. A few days later the two met again. Malesherbes embraced the pastor and presented him to the host of the inn, who revealed the identity of his distinguished guest. At this, Malesherbes exclaimed: "Behold the most obliging man in the world! After a single conversation, he wished to obtain for me the title and salary of a minister, a minister of the Holy Gospel." The pastor was not disconcerted, and replied: "Monsieur de Malesherbes, enlightenment and probity are necessary for one who is to direct souls; Europe credits you with these virtues, and the holy ministry which I offered you would have been well filled."

Later Malesherbes went to Holland, where he was particularly impressed by the gardens, and he brought back with him many specimens for his own estate. For a time after his return he was in Paris only occasionally, and passed the greater part of his days at Malesherbes. The reason for this retreat was not a political one, but a tragedy in his own family—the death of his wife.

At the time of their marriage, Mademoiselle de la Reynière had been a young woman of great beauty and esprit, and sensitive to a marked degree. She was considerably younger than her husband, and her interests were not the same as his. As she grew older her restlessness increased, and she became morose and excitable. From the time of his entrance into the ministry with Turgot, Malesherbes had expressed anxiety about his wife's state of mind. One day in January, 1777, she left the house early in the morning to hunt, as had been her custom for years. By late afternoon she had not returned. A search was begun and, at last, she was found. She had tied her gun to a branch of a tree, attached a blue ribbon to the trigger, adjusted the muzzle to her breast, and ended her unhappiness.

The tragedy plunged Malesherbes into the depths of despair. He accused himself of having given too much thought to public affairs and too little attention to the interests and concerns of his wife. His friends came to him and besought him to come to Paris. But he preferred to remain in the country in the company of his daughter and his grandchildren who became his devoted companions. In the midst of his sorrow he received a message that must have seemed to him to have come from another and very remote world. It was from Rousseau. The letter is, in fact, Rousseau's last epistle to his generous benefactor: "I have heard with very real sorrow, Monsieur, of the loss that you have suffered. To the usual sentiments with which Madame de Malesherbes inspired those who had the honor of knowing her, I add a special sense of gratitude for the kindly welcome that she gave me. The thing that makes her memory all the more precious to me is the fact that she never simulated or deceived. It is sweet to receive in adversity the assurance of devoted hearts, and I have felt that I could at least give you that sort of consolation, the only thing, alas! that I have to offer."

Four years later Malesherbes was bereft of Turgot. In

April, 1776, when they had separated, Turgot had resented the resignation of his associate and had felt that it was premature. But soon afterwards their friendly relations were resumed, and, in token of their reconciliation, Turgot had frequently sent him seeds and rare plants. After Turgot's death, Malesherbes undertook the task of arranging the letters and papers which were left behind. Among them he found a copy of the letter which Turgot had written to the King upon accepting the post of controller-general, and he attached a note to it which read:

Nothing could be more touching than this letter; nothing could give a nobler and finer impression of the character of this minister and, even, of that of the King to whom he had dared write such a note.

The family should preserve it carefully in their archives; I do not see any harm in allowing those friends who may be trusted to make a copy of it. I acknowledge to the family that I have made one for myself and that I will give it to the Marquis Turgot and to the Duchesse de Saint-Aignan if they demand it. But I confess I should like to keep it.

Nevertheless, at present, this letter should not be divulged. It is always unwise to publish documents of this sort that relate to very recent occurrences. I believe that some day this letter will be known through the copies which the family shall have allowed, and that it will be passed on to posterity.

Although he was only sixty-three years of age, Malesherbes, by this time, was beginning to look like an old man. Due to his relentless habit of studying late into the night, his sight was failing. He was oppressed by the sense of the losses which he had sustained, and he was becoming alarmed by the rumblings of discontent, echoes of which penetrated even to his old gray-stone house in the country. To divert himself he plunged into his studies with which his daughter, Madame de Rosambo, helped him. He was no longer the magistrate, but more than ever the country gentleman and the scholar. When he was not in his study he could be found pottering around in his gardens, clad in a brown coat with huge pockets, great gold buttons, and muslin cuffs. His jabot was often speckled with snuff or tobacco, and his round peruke, not always carefully combed, was frequently awry. During this period he published a number of tracts on forestry and on methods for promoting agriculture in France.* A collection of notes in the archives at Tocqueville would seem to indicate that, at this time, he began work on an annotated edition of Pliny the Elder. This project may have been abandoned because of the appearance of an edition of Pliny by Poincinet de Sivry. He also wrote a treatise on the arts and crafts of the Indians in the Carolinas and in Florida. And the work on the *Herbier* continued.

Occasionally there were brief expeditions to Paris in the company of Madame de Rosambo. In the capital he resumed, for a few days, the life that he had followed while he was minister. But he refrained from visiting the Court at Versailles. Artists, scholars, and writers crowded to his house. He boasted that he had met the great Franklin, who had expressed admiration for him. He discussed philosophy with the Abbé Morellet, whose friendship he had won during the Abbé's sojourn in the Bastille, by sending him, as consolation, Hume's *History,* a Tacitus, and Stahl's *Experimenta et observationes chemicæ.* Often he attended

* *Mémoires sur l'administration forestière et sur les qualités individuelles des bois indigènes qui sont acclimatés en France; Mémoires sur les moyens d'accélérer en France les progrès de l'économie sociale; Mémoires sur les moyens d'utiliser les landes en France.*

vaudeville, to which he was devoted. Collé, one of the most popular writers of vaudeville, he considered as a friend. He was a frequent spectator of the balloon ascensions of the Montgolfiers, in whose experiments he evinced a lively interest. To Boissy d'Anglas he wrote enthusiastically: "You can hardly know how happy I am at what your friends' discovery is doing in France. I shall always be grateful to them for what they have gained over the English. . . . It is much better than a victory on the sea, and not a single life has been lost."

While he continued to observe his rule of abstention from public life in Paris, he found it impossible to avoid being drawn into the discussions that were agitating the land. His advancing years and his experience made him the sage of the countryside. And he was a genial sage; there was now neither animus nor bitterness in the opinions which he expressed. After a few years he began to follow with interest the efforts which were being made by successive statesmen to avoid the disaster that seemed to be coming. Necker aroused in him only a slight sympathy: "Il est trop homme d'affaires." Also, he had a shrewd suspicion that the Geneva banker wished to become a dictator. For Calonne who shortly afterward took up the reins he had only contempt. What he had observed during these years convinced him that the key to all reform lay in the nobility. There was the greatest wealth; there, too, were the exemptions and privileges which were depriving the country of a chance for recovery. "I am always the enemy of any aristocracy which interferes with the welfare of the nation," he said. At the same time he was fair-minded enough to add that his first prejudices against the noblesse de l'épée may have come from the fact that he himself originated from the noblesse de robe. It was while pondering the situation of the nobility that he was moved to address to the King the most extraordinary communication that had yet come from his hand—the *Mémoire sur les nobles.*

In the old days, he wrote, the nobles had been exempted from taxation because of their military profession, since as leaders of the army they protected the nation. But now this high purpose had been lost sight of. The exemptions had been granted for services performed; a noble was secure in his privileged state, except in case of distress in the nation or dishonorable conduct. Both these situations now existed, Malesherbes declared. An unworthy noble should be classified like any other person and taxed. For good reason the King might declare a noble and his family to have fallen from their estate. For equally good reason he might later reinstate them. The privileges attendant upon nobility should be dependent upon the virtue and honor of each noble and his services to the country. In recent times, moreover, the nobility had changed. "Many persons have been granted patents of nobility together with the usual privileges. These persons have continued to follow their former trades and businesses and have paid no taxes. Again, there have been nobles of ancient lineage who have gone into commerce and trade and have amassed considerable fortunes. All these persons should be taxed in the same fashion as all others who indulge in business affairs." Malesherbes recommended a careful study of the nobility and the regime of privilege in the hope of bringing about a complete readjustment of the social and economic practices in France. The Mémoire was presented, however, at a time when both King and government were too distraught to heed it, even had they really wished to do so.

———————————

THE retirement of Turgot had given Maurepas complete control of the government. At first there had been a period of reaction from Turgot's economic program and liberal policies. This lasted until June, 1777, when Maurepas found himself forced to recommend the appointment of another Director of Finances. Reluctantly he suggested to Louis XVI the name of Jacques Necker. Being a Genevan and a Protestant, Necker could not be given the title of minister.

The new Director of Finances had come to his post with a considerable reputation behind him. He was known as a financial wizard; he had increased his fortune by successful speculations on the chances of peace in 1763. He was believed to be an admirer of the philosophes, and he was famed for his Friday dinners where Madame Necker presided over a table at which were seated literary lights and savants. In spite of his general reputation for wide knowledge, Jacques Necker knew only money and banking and very little of Courts and politics. That is why he entered upon his duties with the sublime confidence that he could reconcile divided interests in France and abolish extravagance. His coming to power was acclaimed with great enthusiasm; he was greeted as a second Colbert! But within a short time Necker was secretly negotiating loans

from the city of Paris and from towns within the pays
d'état.

Nevertheless, Necker was not an administrator of the
old school. He tried to enforce some of Turgot's reforms
that had never been put into effect. He reduced the number of farmers-general in the provinces, and he persuaded
the King to abolish feudalism on the royal domains. He
also got under way a plan for the establishment of Estates
in the provinces. But Necker was still far from his goal,
and he had a stubborn nobility against him.

By the year 1781 he felt that he was blocked. In an effort
to save his plans he persuaded Louis XVI to consent to the
publication of the *Compte rendu au Roi par M. Necker.*
The nation had never had revealed to it the extent of its
credits and debits, and it had never actually been shown
where the money went that should have been used to pay
off debts. It was Necker's belief that his cause would be
strengthened by an exposé of the miserable situation. In
this opinion he was wholly mistaken; the revelation increased the alarm of the privileged classes for their own
security. Economy was impossible and, some of them argued, unnecessary; on sea and on land France was regain-
ing her lost reputation by her successful intervention in
the cause of the American colonies.

What many failed to see was the fact that these efforts
and these victories cost money. Necker was treated as an
alarmist and was condemned by the Court for putting
within every man's reach the secret of government finances. Maurepas was furious at his action and ridiculed
the *Compte rendu,* calling it the *Conte bleu.* Parlement refused to register his edict establishing Estates in the province of Bourbonnais. And when Louis XVI declined to

grant him the title of minister, Necker withdrew. To the liberals, May 19, 1781, the day of his retirement, was a day of discouragement and mourning.

Necker's failure hastened the debacle. Even the pleasant and always obliging Calonne, who soon came to power, could not maintain himself for long. He had not the favor of the King, but he enjoyed the confidence of the King's brother, Charles of Artois, of the Polignacs, and of many of the grands seigneurs. They felt that he would be a safe man; he would not have the force of Maupeou or the pig-headedness of Turgot.

Calonne's policy, at first, was to spend lavishly and to float loans and lotteries. In the beginning, a good harvest and the success of the American enterprise helped him. But soon loans became increasingly difficult to negotiate, and Parlement refused to register new taxes. At length, Calonne was forced to fall back on Turgot's measure and advocate the equalization of taxes. He knew, indeed, that Parlement would refuse this proposal as vigorously as it had all the others. He suggested, therefore, another expedient to the King—to go back to the precedent of 1624 and call an Assembly of Notables.

This plan was virtually a confession of failure on the part of the minister. There were many who did not believe in it. Malesherbes exclaimed: "Why not the Estates-General?" And he hastened to Versailles for an audience with the King. Louis XVI, however, seemed to be entirely incapable of coming to any decision, while Calonne who, like many others, feared the Estates, was now in a mood to be as stubborn as Turgot had been. One hundred and forty-seven members were selected by Calonne and his friends. Among them were prelates who were hostile to him and a number of magistrates whose support he hoped to gain by the honor which he had conferred on them. From the remainder he expected to win a sure majority. On February 22, 1786, Calonne's wish was fulfilled: the Notables assembled. It was an odd assortment of prelates, grands seigneurs, intendants and counselors of State, and deputies from the pays d'état and the larger towns. It was unwieldy and useless. It might have done much for France had it consented to fiscal equality; but neither of the two privileged classes would consent to its own taxation, and the revolutionary tone of Calonne's remarks alarmed the more conservative members of the assembly. In April, 1787, Calonne left his post and his country. Behind him there was a record of complete failure, and yet, unwittingly, he had accomplished one important thing—he had placed before a body that was supposedly representative of the nation the matter of fiscal equality. Most intelligent Frenchmen were now debating, one way or the other, this important question. Calonne's tactics and their collapse, too, had made Louis XVI thoroughly alive to the necessity for immediate reform. The King was desperately in need of a leader. Turgot was dead. With many misgivings, he turned to a prelate, Loménie de Brienne, Archbishop of Toulouse.

The choice of De Brienne was not a surprise to France. In a day when fame, thanks to the advertisement of friends at Court, was easily obtained, he was reputed to be a man of considerable ability and ingenuity. He was well connected and he was not unfriendly to the new philosophy. There was not much of the priest in him, and there was considerably more of the cultured gentleman of the world. He had traveled a great deal, and his journeys had not always been in the direction of Rome. In his archiepiscopal palace he had a laboratory where he dabbled occasionally in scientific experiments, and he was approved by many liberals for his opposition to the religious orders. All the past history of this very versatile person led some to hope that De Brienne would be able to better the situation.

The beginnings of his administration were encouraging. De Brienne's first move was to associate Chancellor Lamoignon with himself in the council. The chancellor was a cousin of Malesherbes and a man who, for personal reasons, was eager for a bout with the refractory Parlement. It was hoped to make De Brienne's council a ministry of reconciliation and to call into it men of all shades of opinion but men who could be controlled. Among them was Malesherbes, who was selected because of his reputation and his age. He was persuaded to accept only with the greatest difficulty. He was obdurate and almost disagreeable about it. To his cousin, the chancellor, he remarked: "A magistrate who has made war on ministers should never be a minister himself." Finally he agreed to join them, but only on condition that he should become a minister without portfolio. "I did not have any function"; he commented later, "I had only the right to speak my own mind, and, you may be sure, what I said was not published." Court gossip had it that Malesherbes did nothing but exercise to the limit his gift as a raconteur and that his endless anecdotes interfered with the business of the council.

But while he had no department of his own, Malesherbes' time was occupied usefully. He resumed at once some of the labors which he had abandoned in April, 1776. Within a short time he presented to the King and council recommendations for the toleration of the Protestants. When asked by one who was not a sympathizer why he persisted in this interest, Malesherbes replied curtly: "It is the least that I can do to make reparation to the Protestants for all the evil that my uncle, Monsieur de Basville, did them in Languedoc." If mercy and reparation were one cause for his resuming the agitation for toleration, there was still another. To Rabaut Saint-Étienne he had written: "After all, it is unjust to demand of everyone a blind docility—an unquestioning submission to the orders of the priest."

In the cause of the Protestants he went to great pains to examine the laws of Louis XIV. He pointed out the fact that the present policy of the government went far beyond the original intentions of the ordinances, and he stressed the importance to the State of a policy of religious toleration: "Heretics should be only a sect in the Church and not a party in the State. . . . It is just and necessary to give to Protestants, who are subjects of the King, a civil status and the common rights of all citizens." He declared himself in favor of the marriage of Protestant and Catholic. But he did not confine his demands for toleration to the followers of the reformed religion; he interceded for the Quakers, the Anabaptists, the Mussulmen, and the Jews. Concerning the Jews, there are several dossiers of notes which he made in preparation for his plea on their behalf. From these it is evident that he made a careful study of their history, their laws and ethics, and their customs. Some of his information he passed on to the Marquis de Mirabeau, who was, at this time, carrying on a campaign in their behalf. In his own Mémoire Malesherbes presented a detailed statement of their situation and of their psychology. He asserted that their exclusion from rights, professions, and even ordinary protection was responsible, in great part, for the unfortunate characteristics that sometimes marked their race. He showed them to be a hardworking and laborious people. Like the philosophes, he abominated persecution of all dissident religious opinions, but with him it was not only for mercy's sake but also for reasons of State: "The authority of the government over the various sects should be confined to preventing them from becoming parties within the State; each time that you begin a persecution you unite them into strong groups which present a serious obstacle to the authority of the government."

At last Malesherbes had the reward of his efforts. In January, 1787, an edict of toleration for the members of the reformed religion was registered by Parlement. Their civil disabilities were removed, their marriages validated, and they were granted complete liberty to participate fully in the professions and in trade. Encouraged by this unexpected success, Malesherbes attempted once more to assert himself in regard to national affairs, and he addressed to the council a *Mémoire sur la situation actuelle des affaires*.

The difficulties with which De Brienne found himself confronted had served as the occasion for the memorandum. De Brienne had failed to get his projects through the Notables, and that body had been dismissed. Now he knew no way to solve the economic difficulty other than that of increasing the taxes. There again he ran up against the stone wall of the Parlement. In the course of the struggle with the magistrates Louis XVI had stood by his minister, and in August, 1787, he had exiled the Parlement to Troyes. But this move had done no good, for the provin-

cial tribunals had refused to register the decrees. In this re-
solve they had been strengthened by the support of the
people who were, by now, exasperated by the rapid succession of proposals for increased taxation and the failure
to persuade the two upper Estates to submit to taxation.
To destroy this alliance of Parlement and people, the government proposed to reform the entire system of the courts.
It was the old situation of 1771 all over again. Once more
Malesherbes' sympathies were not with the government,
and he stated his case briefly and succinctly in his Mémoire
of 1787. He blamed the King and the ministers for the de-
plorable situation, and he called for an honest statement
of the situation to the King. "One recalls," he wrote, "that
the King came to the throne with a formal project for
economies, but one realizes that never has the extravagance of ruling gone so far as it has today. . . . In earlier
times it was the Parlement that aroused the public; now
it is the public that excites the Parlement, and both are
serious. . . . This is a truth which must be revealed to the
King in all its details and without concealing anything, because whatever we do today will have either fortunate or
fatal results for the realm. Today it is not a question of
quieting a momentary crisis, but rather of putting out a
spark which may produce a conflagration. . . . You will
say that the danger which I prophesy is not near at hand.
Whoever says that seems to me to be very foolish. . . .
Often, in the past, we have reproached old ministers of
young kings for holding to such an idea and for having
shown a culpable indifference to future calamities which
they themselves would not live to witness. I myself do not
wish to merit that reproach. . . . It is intolerable to take
any more of the substance of the people to pay for useless

expenses. That is what will cause the resentment of the people and we should tell the King that this resentment is justifiable."

The Mémoire concluded by calling for economies in the Royal Household and in government, and advising the convocation of the Estates-General as a proof of good faith with the people and the only means of providing relief for the deficit.

This was Malesherbes' last warning before the storm broke. He saw the future so very clearly. But his advice was ignored, and when the Estates were called, it was not recognized as part of Malesherbes' program, for he had retired. He had seen many of the methods which, when President of the Cour des Aides, he had opposed, put into operation. He wrote that he could not, with a clear conscience, remain in a ministry of whose methods he disapproved.

Another struggle ensued between De Brienne and the Parlement with the result that, on May 8, 1788, the suppression of the courts was decreed.

The magistrates were now out of the way; they retired to their homes to realize a little later how great had been their contribution to the Revolution. On July 5 it was announced that the Estates-General would be called. In August the government officially acknowledged its bankruptcy, and Loménie de Brienne withdrew. Only a little while afterwards it became known that Monsieur Necker would be given another chance to show what he could do.

CHAPTER VIII

OBSERVATIONS ON THE
REVOLUTION

FROM August, 1788, the approaching meeting of the Estates-General was the principal topic of conversation in almost every salon, café, and shop. The Estates had not met since 1614, and people in general were ignorant of their real character. Everyone had his own opinion. There were some who were convinced that they knew the facts, and they gave France the rather doubtful benefit of their knowledge. Pamphlets were the media for spreading their opinions. Others orated or discussed the subject before enthralled listeners in the cafés near the Palais-Royal. Many of them did not give the same answer as the Abbé Sieyès. His reply was simple: "The Estates-General is the Third Estate."

The question that aroused the greatest difference of opinion was the one concerning the form of the Estates and how they should meet. It had been decided by the government that a larger representation should be allowed the Third Estate; a decree of the council issued in December, 1788, had declared that the Third Estate should have as many representatives as the two higher estates combined. But, some asked, is this sufficient, and does this arrangement settle everything? Malesherbes soon found himself involved in the controversy that arose over these matters.

Thanks to the fact that he had been among the earliest, if not the very first, of his generation to have publicly suggested the recall of the Estates-General, Malesherbes was regarded as a leading authority on the subject. His house in the Quartier du Marais became the scene of many discussions and debates. He was consulted by the disciples of the philosophes, all of whom wished reform but few of whom desired revolution. Pamphleteers, too, sought his advice. Boissy d'Anglas visited him frequently during the winter of 1788, and Rabaut Saint-Étienne, upholder of the *bourgeois patriots,* wrote him often from Nîmes. Malesherbes had very definite ideas on the subject, but before exposing them he decided to write them down and present them as suggestions to the King.

In this letter, the last known Mémoire from his hand, one finds the fully developed idea of monarchy as Malesherbes knew it and as he believed that monarchy and the Estates should be. The first impulse toward such a conception had come from his reading of Fénelon. In his younger days *Télémaque* had been his political bible. Then his views were further developed by his contact with the philosophes. Finally they had been tempered and tested by his long experience in the Cour des Aides, whose selfish interests he had left behind him, and by more recent observations during his service in the ministries of Turgot and De Brienne. His ideas were challenged by many of his friends and by at least one member of his family.

Unlike his intimates and relations, Malesherbes recognized that the summoning of the Estates-General would create a revolution: "A great revolution is about to give back to the French monarchy all its glory. A people that have been too long deprived of the faculty of defending their own cause are about to be reinstated in the most sacred of their rights."

He then proceeds to an examination of the character of the Estates. Shall they be as they have been in the past, or is it necessary that they be changed to meet new conditions? "Shall the Estates observe the precedents of earlier times? There are many reasons for believing that such a procedure would not be the right one to follow. Since their last meeting in 1614, other provinces have been added to France, the existence of landed proprietors has created an abuse of many privileges and exemptions, and there has been a considerable elevation of intelligence among one class of citizens which, for too long, has counted for nothing in the nation's affairs."

This class, he wrote, must be heard. And to be heard, it must be protected against being submerged and oppressed by the higher classes. There must be a unity of spirit and of purpose among all classes that are included in the Estates: "The prelate, the gentleman, the magistrate, and the small landowner must now see only the nation in its affliction; and each should make every possible sacrifice in order to give us again the strength of a flourishing state. . . . This is no time to depend for our decision on charters that were made in earlier times."

Malesherbes saw only one way to follow if success was to be certain; the Estates-General must meet as one body in one house. This was, after all, merely the logical outcome of his idea of the nation. Having denied the necessity of orders in society, he could scarcely have approved of the continuance of the three separate Estates. And for this idea he fought among his friends and acquaintances.

In this regard he often found himself more in sympathy with the pamphleteers than with the members of his family. His relative, Paul de Rosambo, for example, wrote him that such an arrangement would "démonarchiser la monarchie." But Malesherbes stood his ground. He had come to believe, he wrote, in a social contract. It was, however, far different from that of his protégé, Jean Jacques Rousseau; Malesherbes' idea of a social contract was expressed, in his letter to the King, in the following words: "Nevertheless, a contract exists, but it is one which reposes on good faith: 'Make us happy and we will make you powerful, protect our property and we will protect your domains. Do not allow anyone to touch us and we will defend you to the last drop of our blood. Give us enlightened and incorruptible judges, and we will submit to your decisions. Do not set in advance the tribute that we owe you when your revenues are not sufficient to allow you to repulse the enemy, to keep up the necessary forces, and to avenge offenses committed against the nation, and we will manage to give you every penny that a justifiable attack and a necessary defense demand.' This law, dictated by nature, confirmed by reason, will be forever the bond which, in monarchies, unites subjects and sovereign. No monarch has the power to destroy it, and it would be madness to try to weaken it."

Could anything be a more typical expression of eighteenth-century political idealism in France? Malesherbes, then, was not willing to cross the Channel or the Atlantic for a remedy. It could be found at home in the traditions and original sanctions of the French people.

But the Mémoire contained more than theory. The remaining sections suggested a plan for the election and procedure of the Estates-General. Throughout it is evident that Malesherbes was trying to provide a system which would give every advantage and every freedom to the Third Estate. To expedite the work of the Estates, for

REVOLUTION   125

haste, he believed, was necessary, he proposed their division into eleven committees, each one to consider some special problem related to the business of reform with which France was confronted.

The recommendations contained in the Mémoire were not accepted. Perhaps it was foreknowledge of this which prompted Malesherbes to decline the King's expressed desire that he take an active part in the deliberations of the Estates once they had convened. On the occasion of this interview with Louis XVI, Malesherbes presented the Mémoire. In the course of the conversation he gave the King a grave warning which was couched in the frankest of terms. He recalled the fate of Charles I of England, "who came either too early or too late." The same issues, royal prerogative and popular right, he said, were now at stake. And unless Louis XVI decided beforehand how far he ought to go, the people might take his rights away from him. "The success of this plan [the Estates-General] depends upon your firm resolves. Without these, one cannot tell what will happen. It will not go as far as it did with Charles I, but I would not undertake to say what other excesses might occur. You must be prepared, Sire, to prevent them."

Instead, Louis XVI came to few decisions, he was not prepared, and when the Estates-General convened they met separately and at Versailles.

ABOUT the first of May, 1789, the members of the three Estates began assembling at Versailles. They brought with them their *cahiers de doléances,* the books of complaints and recommendations that each deputy was instructed to bring from his district. Many of these books expressed the same complaints and suggestions for the reason that some were copied from model cahiers drawn up by liberal writers and pamphleteers while others had been influenced by the network of masonic and other secret societies which abounded in France at this time. Another important model was the Remonstrances of the various courts of Parlement. These were always printed and distributed, and a great many of these earlier complaints were reproduced verbatim in the cahiers of 1789.

Like every public figure who had been interested in the cause of reform, Malesherbes had his part in the writing of cahiers not only from his own province but also from other districts of France. His correspondence shows that he gave advice for the cahiers from Langres, where Paul de Rosambo was living at the time, and also from Nîmes, where Rabaut Saint-Étienne was one of the leading figures in the preparation of the doléances. In these instances, Malesherbes' suggestions were exactly in line with what he had expressed in his Remonstrances and later Mémoires to the King; a single assembly, fiscal equality, abolition of lettres de cachet, and complete religious toleration.

For a few days after the opening of the Estates-General enthusiasm and a sentiment of good will prevailed. Louis XVI was proclaimed the Restorer of French Liberty. His portrait appeared along with Washington and Franklin as one of the three liberators of the century. But the scene changed in a fashion as abrupt as it was devastating. Due, in part, to his own uncertainty, the King soon began to vacillate between attempts at reaction and sudden enthusiasms for liberty. These frequent changes and contradictions bred distrust. To his people and even to his entourage Louis XVI became an enigma. Economic crisis, public suspicion, a selfish nobility, and the fashionable philosophic doctrines, combined with the weakness of the King, contributed largely to his rapid decline.

The storm began with the Tennis Court Oath, which resulted in the transformation of the Estates-General into a National Assembly of one house. It continued with the rising of July 14 in Paris and the frenzied session of the night of August 4 and 5 at Versailles when the nobility, in their alarm, abandoned their feudal rights, hunting rights and exemptions from taxation, while the curés yielded their tithes and fees. But this was to no avail. Suspicion and hatred, born in part of the timidity of the King and in part of the general distrust of his entourage of nobles and armed forces, led to the days of October when the Paris mob made monarchy and assembly captive and carried them off to Paris. It was the climax in the first act of the tragedy.

After that event, the King was virtually a prisoner of the Commune of Paris. A brief respite followed, and during this time Louis XVI made every effort to regain the confidence of his subjects. But this was difficult to do, for his courtiers were beginning to emigrate and were spreading over Europe the news of the plight of their King. By their actions Louis XVI became the victim of the emigration. Finally, in June, 1791, deserted by his closest friends and fearful of the popular clamor, the King tried to join his absent nobles and their armies. The flight of the King to Varennes was the most pathetically stupid thing that could have been invented, and the journey back to Paris made the monarchy ridiculous.

This second return to the capital had a far greater significance than the first; it marked the definite break of the more radical liberals with the King. In their eyes he was no longer the patriot but the traitor. He had to accept the Constitution of 1791 which gave him practically no right but the dangerous one of a suspensive veto. In September of this same year, the Constitution was put into operation, and the King found himself confronted with a Legislative Assembly two-thirds of which were new men. Most of them were unknown to him, and he regarded the great number as radicals, whether they were Jacobins, Cordeliers, or Girondists.

Sometimes from the country, more frequently now from Paris, Malesherbes watched the events of these three years. At first, even he had been filled with hope. In spite of all his own experiences and in spite of the fact that Louis XVI had not heeded his warning and had not prepared his policy in advance of the Estates-General, Malesherbes, for a moment, felt that the experiment might succeed. Although he regretted the angry scenes that preceded it, he rejoiced when the Tennis Court Oath prepared the way for the transformation of the Estates-General into a National Assembly. That change had always been his wish. But the outburst of July alarmed him, and when October came, bringing with it the transference of the King and assembly to Paris by the mob, Malesherbes began to despair. He saw in it the beginning of the fulfilment of his prophecies. He had warned the King, but, at the same time, he had reassured him that things would not go so far as they had with Charles of England. Now he was not so sure that the monarchy was safe. "Ce pauvre Roy,"

Moleville reports him as saying, "I pity him indeed. I fear that he will have a hard time escaping those scoundrels, and it is a shame, for he is a worthy prince. . . . But in certain situations, like the present one, for instance, the qualities that are virtues in a private citizen become almost vices in a person who occupies the throne; they may be good for the other world, but they are worth nothing in this one." He did not doubt the honesty and good intentions of Louis XVI, and he believed that the King's mistakes came from timidity and a lack of self-confidence.

More and more as the tragedy approached its inevitable conclusion, Malesherbes felt himself drawn to the King. He began attending Court more frequently. "Although I hate to dress myself up and although I abominate that cursed sword which gets between my legs when I go upstairs and which will make me break my neck some day, I attend the King's levée regularly every Sunday. For the greatest pleasure of the whole week is when I see with my own eyes that this brav homme is well. I never talk to him, but that is nothing; it is enough for me to have seen him, and I think, too, that he is glad to have seen me there."

By 1792, Malesherbes was thoroughly aware that he was witnessing the end of the monarchy, but he was not yet sure in what form the end would come. There is evidence, too, in his letters that he began to regret the passing of those things which, in earlier times, he had condemned. When Edward Gibbon wrote him requesting an explanation of the term "princes of the blood," Malesherbes replied with a letter in which there was a distinctly wistful note. In other parts of his correspondence there were unmistakable signs of discouragement and even, at times, of scorn. To Roland, the Girondist minister, he wrote in 1790: "In times like these, when violent passions rule the world, it is better not to let reason speak. It would even harm reason to allow it utterance, for its words would never be heard; the enthusiasts would excite the people against the very truths that, at another time, would have been received with general approbation." The close of the year 1791 found him in a mood of complete disapproval. Many of the principles for which he had fought in the past had been traduced and misinterpreted, he wrote. When the Civil Constitution of the Clergy, which required of all ecclesiastics an oath of obedience and created a State Church, was passed, Malesherbes was as much distressed as the King. But the reasons for their distress were different; Malesherbes had stood for toleration, but he saw in this law the means for instituting a policy of intolerance toward Catholics.

In brief, Malesherbes' liberalism was the indigenous liberalism of the philosophes. It was not the republicanism of the Jacobin or the Girondist, or the American formulæ as interpreted by Brissot and the future deputy Thomas Paine. Malesherbes had once declared that he was the enemy of aristocracy when it interfered with the welfare of the State; now to Boissy d'Anglas he asserted the same principle and applied it to the leaders of the Revolution: "I am the first enemy of any aristocracy—meaning a government where a certain number of men seize an authority not given to them or a greater authority than that which was given them. I cannot approve it without being untrue to my professed principles nor can I refuse to say what I think without being faithless to my character. I have not expressed myself in public . . . because popular passion is at such a point that whatever I said or did, even to the extent of dying for it, would do no good. . . . I do not aspire to the glory of being either legislator, reformer, or restorer of my country. I am too old. I hope to end my days in silence and obscurity."

Nevertheless, Malesherbes did not remain entirely silent. When the crisis of the spring of 1792 was reached and when Louis XVI, at bay, dared to exercise his veto on the laws against the nonjuring clergy and emigrant nobles, and dismissed the Roland ministry, Malesherbes did not hesitate to give him encouragement. And the threatening scenes of June 20, when the mob invaded the Tuileries and violated the dignity of the monarchy, did not deter him from proffering his willingness to help in whatever way he could.

He was traveling in Switzerland when the news of the riot reached him. Suddenly, one morning, he appeared at the house of the Marquise d'Aguesseau, a relative. "I am leaving for Paris," he announced. "The situation is very grave. I am returning to my post. Perhaps the King will need me."

It is unlikely that Malesherbes had, at this time, any idea of the enormous responsibility that would shortly come to him, but he felt the duty of being near his distraught monarch, to counsel and to encourage him if occasion offered. He approved the King's reluctance to go to war against the European Allies who, seeing the danger to their systems of government, were preparing to invade France. And when the Jacobins, stung to fury by Brunswick's defiance and threats to France and inspired by Danton's flaming oratory, planned to call out the mob and put an end to this royal traitor, Malesherbes sought to warn his master. Through Girondist leaders who believed him to be in closer touch with the King than he actually was, Malesherbes had foreknowledge of the conspiracy. He hastened to the Tuileries with the news. But Louis XVI refused to heed the warning, because, as he said, the only way to prevent the scheme was to use force and to shed blood. The reply to Malesherbes' message was tragic: "I cannot change my mind on the proposition of the Girondists; I am not the less grateful to Monsieur de Malesherbes. You will tell him of my gratitude without delay."

Nothing was done, then, and rumors continued to spread in Paris. It was even averred that Louis XVI was secretly gathering arms and men in the Tuileries for an attack on the government. Bretons and men of Marseilles paraded the streets. It was a good preparation for August 10 when the tocsin would sound. At its notes, the various sections of Paris took possession of the Hotel de Ville while the mob began marching on the Tuileries. To save his family and in the vain hope of avoiding bloodshed, Louis XVI finally accepted the advice of Roederer, Procureur-Général of the Department of Paris, and with the Queen, the *enfants de France,* and Madame Elizabeth went to the Manège where the Legislative Assembly was sitting. From that place the King sent a hurried message to the guards at the Tuileries ordering them to cease firing. But the message was not delivered. Within two hours eight hundred of the guards had been killed and of the attackers there were about four hundred killed and wounded.

Louis XVI was now guilty of shedding the blood of

Frenchmen. The Legislative Assembly deposed the King and ordered the election of a National Convention to determine upon a new government for France.

On Friday, September 21, the Legislative Assembly dissolved itself with the words of François de Neufchâteau: "The Legislative Assembly is no more; the Convention assumes control. We are glad, upon withdrawing, to promise an absolute obedience to any laws that it passes."

This day was also marked by the arrival of exciting news from the front. The battle of Valmy had been fought and won; France was relieved from the immediate danger of further invasion by the European Allies. On September 22, in the midst of great rejoicing, the monarchy was abolished, and the day was decreed to be the first day of the First Year in the life of the French Republic. This act was acclaimed as a sure sign of the establishment of internal peace. It was believed that Frenchmen would unite in a feast of brotherhood and equality. As a matter of fact, the proclamation of a new state of things brought to a head the struggle of Jacobin and Girondist for control. This contention centered, at first, about the person of Louis XVI.

The Girondists, who were cautious, favored a policy of leniency toward the royal captive by reason of the soothing effect that such an attitude would have on the nations of Europe that had not yet joined the Allies. But Danton, Robespierre, and the Jacobins favored the defiance of Europe by the destruction of the King. Both parties agreed that some decisive step was necessary. Louis in France was more than an encumbrance; his presence was a menace to the Republic and as long as he lived he would be a rallying point for nobles and for all other discontented Frenchmen. And Louis in Europe might be equally dangerous; naturally all the crowned heads of the Continent saw in his peril the possibility of a similar fate for themselves. As long as he existed he would be a living reminder of their own danger. But the principal bone of contention was how to proceed. The King was an anachronism; legally, he no longer existed. He was a prisoner charged with crime and traitorous action. But, how to judge him? Could he be judged? In the penal code there was nothing about what to do with a traitorous tyrant, and nature, that divine authority for so many spirits of the eighteenth century, appeared to have taught mercy. This was embarrassing. Robespierre suggested a simple and typical solution: "There will be no trial. Louis XVI is not even accused. The people do not judge as courts do; they do not deliver sentences . . ., they launch the bolt; they do not condemn kings, they destroy them."

There were many who did not agree with these remarks, but the fact remained that the case of Capet must be settled and Capet himself disposed of. He was a menace to internal peace and to external security. At last it was decided that the Convention should undertake the trial. When this agreement was reached the *conventionnels* had to listen to tedious sermons on the decorum and dignity that they should observe during the proceedings. The words were wasted; when the time came they did not observe them.

Once the matter of a trial was settled, everyone was eager for haste; the sooner the thing was done the better. On December 3, the Convention as a court was presented with the *Acte énonciatif des crimes de Louis Capet*. On December 11, the prisoner was brought to the bar of the Convention. He displayed no emotion and showed a clear head when, according to the custom, the charges were read and he was asked to respond to them. Forty-three questions in the form of accusations were put to him. He denied them all. They ranged from general charges of conspiracy against the Revolution and plots with foreign powers to participation in the instigation of riots in Nîmes and Montauban. To the last question: "Louis, have you anything to add?" he replied: "I request a copy of this *Acte* and the communication of all the evidence against me, and that I be accorded counsel to take charge of my case." The prisoner was then returned to the Temple.

On December 12, a deputation of the conventionnels went to the prison and informed the King that he would be allowed to select his defenders and that the Convention would proceed to the trial without delay. Taken by surprise, for he had expected to be given time to deliberate on his choice, Louis XVI first selected Target, a lawyer of repute. His choice was wise; Target had been a member of the commission that drew up the Constitution which Louis XVI was charged with having abused. To the astonishment and dismay of the King, Target declined to serve and wrote to the Convention: "A man so liberal and so republican as myself should not accept functions of which he holds himself incapable." He was careful to sign his letter: "Le Républicain Target." In haste, Louis then selected Monsieur Tronchet, a famous lawyer of long-standing reputation in Paris, who had been a deputy to the Estates-General. Tronchet, a fearless old man, reluctantly accepted the task.

In all this time, most of the Royalists had been silent.

CHAPTER IX

IN DEFENSE OF THE KING

Citoyen-Président,

I do not know if the Convention will allow Louis XVI counsel to defend himself and if it will permit him to make his own choice of his defenders. In that case, I wish Louis XVI to know that if he selects me for this task I am ready to accept it. I do not ask you to inform the Convention of my offer, for I am far from believing myself important enough to receive its attention. But twice I was called to serve in the council by him who was once my master, and, in those days, such an honor was coveted by everyone. Now that this task is one which many hold to be dangerous, I feel that I owe him the same service. If I knew how to inform him that I am at his disposal I should not have addressed myself to you. I have thought that you, with your position, would have more means of making my wishes known to him.

With all my respect, Citoyen-Président

I am your very humble and very obedient servant,

LAMOIGNON DE MALESHERBES.

Paris 11 X^bre 1792.

ON the very day when Louis XVI was first brought before the Convention, its presiding officer received this letter. About the same time a number of other offers were made. Some came from obscure persons and some from famous persons in France, others were from England and had been forwarded by Bertrand de Moleville, former Minister of State and at that time an émigré. It is not known how many of these letters were shown to the King. He was told at once, however, of Malesherbes' request, and he accepted it immediately. On December 13 Malesherbes' appointment was announced, and his letter was published in the *Journal des débats et des décrets*. At the same time it became known that Malesherbes had been granted the extraordinary privilege of seeing the King as often as he liked.

On the following day Tronchet and Malesherbes visited their client for the first time. Malesherbes relates that, as he was climbing the Temple stairs for this interview, his knees almost gave way, and he had to rest on a step to keep from fainting. Finally he reached the door of the King's chamber. There Cléry, the faithful secretary, stood. He led Malesherbes into the room.

Louis was sitting at his table, a volume of Tacitus in his hand. As soon as he heard the door open, he rose. When Malesherbes saw the King, his arms outstretched in welcome, coming to meet him, he broke down. It was the King, as always, who was calm and collected. He embraced his old minister and said: "You are not afraid to risk your life in order to save mine; but, my friend, you are making a useless sacrifice." "No, Sire," replied Malesherbes. "I am not exposing my life, and I do not believe that Your Majesty's is in any danger. The cause is just, and the evidence in your defense is so good as to promise a victory."

The interview which followed was carried on with difficulty. It was necessary to move into a small room in the adjoining turret in order to avoid being overheard by the guards who had been stationed on the stairway and in the hall. The King then questioned Malesherbes about his plans and about the others who might be included in the defense. Tronchet was an old lawyer of considerable experience who had been a member and, at one time, Presi-

Malesherbes and Louis Sixteenth in the prison

dent of the National Assembly. Were there any others whom Monsieur de Malesherbes desired, Louis XVI asked. In reply to this question Malesherbes told the King that, in view of the advanced age of his two counselors, they might find it desirable to call in a younger assistant. For the moment, however, the defense would be restricted to Malesherbes and his associate. Tronchet was then introduced, and the King and his two lawyers made a preliminary examination of the charges that the Acte énonciatif contained. They also drew up a provisional plan for the defense. It was Louis XVI himself who suggested the schedule of work that should be followed when he remarked to Malesherbes: "I wish to be alone with you, reviewing our memories and our former conversations; we shall talk of the trial in the evening. . . . Here the pleasures shall be in the morning and business in the evening; it was exactly the contrary at Versailles."

From December 14 to December 26, the day when the trial began, this routine was followed. Every morning Malesherbes climbed the stairs to the King's room in the Temple. He brought with him the notes and suggestions that the defense had worked out the night before. These the King would put aside to study after Malesherbes had left. Meanwhile they discussed the affairs of the day. At the King's request Malesherbes brought him all the papers and journals that he could lay his hands on, for Louis XVI insisted on reading what people were writing about him. They discussed the gossip of the town, and they talked of the past. Malesherbes even read to him some of the Mémoires which Maurepas, in the days of his ministry, had refused to allow the King to see. During one of the first of these morning talks, Louis XVI made a strange demand of Malesherbes. He asked him if he possessed a copy of Hume's *History of the House of Stuart*. When Malesherbes said that he had it in his library, he was asked to bring it with him the next day. Cléry relates that Louis XVI read in it every night before retiring. Malesherbes was charged with all sorts of personal commissions by his client—with seeing that words of comfort were conveyed to the Queen and with carrying messages to the few of his intimates who had dared to remain in Paris. At noon Malesherbes would withdraw to join the King's counsel or else to interview the deputies of the Convention about missing papers. At five o'clock the counselors appeared at the Temple and went over the King's case with him. This conference always ended at nine o'clock in the evening.

In spite of protestations of good intentions on the part of the government, access to the King was not always easy. Often Malesherbes was searched and frequently he was made the object of gibes and insults as he stopped in the guardroom to leave his laissez-passer on entering the building. All of the guards were by no means as sympathetic as Citoyen Lepitre, who, on the day following one of these unfortunate occurrences, approached the old man when he appeared, offered him his hand, and said: "Take courage, Monsieur, I am not one of the great number." To this Malesherbes replied: "Cela me fait du bien. Please conduct me yourself every time that you are on duty when I come to see the King."

At other times his client was the cause of difficulty. There were days when Louis seemed listless and heedless. On one of these occasions Malesherbes left the Temple in dejection and remarked sadly to a loyal guardsman: "I cannot interest His Majesty in his affairs. No matter how serious things are, he shows only the greatest indifference to his fate." In fact, as time went on, Malesherbes came to believe that Louis had failed entirely to grasp the real significance of the Revolution at its beginning and that it was only after his imprisonment that the full gravity of the situation dawned upon him. And when the realization came, it stunned him. To the Abbé Morellet, Malesherbes later reported the following conversation which took place between the King and his counselors in the Temple. They had been talking of the Revolution. Tronchet exclaimed: "Who would have believed that it would have gone so far?" Louis replied: "There was one man who foresaw the danger and who, at the opening of the Estates-General, arranged to have a Mémoire sent to me. He foretold almost everything that might happen, but I did not believe it." At this, the King stopped, regarded Malesherbes, and said: "I think the Mémoire was from you, Monsieur de Malesherbes." It was only then that Malesherbes knew that the King had read his warning.

At the first of these discussions Malesherbes was very insistent that the main point of the defense should be an attack on the competence of the Convention to judge the King, for he knew that many of the conventionnels had already expressed a doubt that they were empowered to act as a court. There was, he argued, no clause in the penal code which gave such a right to any body in France, and, he added, the Convention had not been elected by the people for the purpose of trying the King but only to determine what form of government should be adopted. But Louis XVI was very firm in his opposition to this proposal. He had accepted the competence of the Convention when he appeared before it on December 11. Furthermore, he said, he was innocent, and he preferred to be justified publicly rather than to hide behind *une contestation de compétence*. To Malesherbes this was a disappointment, for the argument appealed to the man of law, but he bowed before the wishes of his royal client. Reluctantly he and Tronchet then turned to an examination of the Acte énonciatif and of the evidence that was offered in support of its charges.

Here Malesherbes' difficulty was not with the King but with the Convention and its committees. The two defenders were convinced that all the evidence had not been communicated to them. Most of the papers that were said to have been found in the safe at the Tuileries were shown them, but Malesherbes believed that there were other papers which might have exculpated the King and that they were being withheld. There was, indeed, one bit of evidence on which he could not lay his fingers. Malesherbes had been in communication with Bertrand de Moleville, who had gathered for him testimony from émigrés and ex-officials then in London. These papers had been dispatched, but they had not been delivered to the defense. He had to go before the committee of the Convention that had charge of the evidence and demand them. Some of them he finally saw, but there was one package for which he asked that he was not allowed to see. They told him that it had been lost.* Thus far Malesherbes and Tronchet had had

---

* In the séance of January 11, 1793, Garat, Minister of Justice, offered another explanation: "You know that we were snowed under with documents of all sorts, most of them insignificant. . . . As to the manuscripts about which Bertrand is complaining, I declare that the committee never had cognizance of them unless, it might be, these papers were enclosed in a package which we did not unseal."

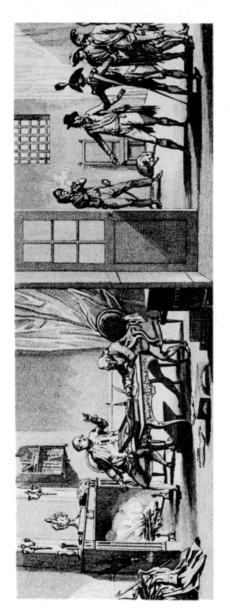

Contemporary engraving showing the King in prison dictating to Malesherbes

communicated to them one hundred and fifty-eight pieces of evidence, but they remained convinced that there were many more. This delay in their delivery worried them. Their impatience and anxiety were increased when, on December 16, they received another communication from the Convention informing them that the King's plea would have to be delivered within ten days.

At once the two lawyers sent a letter of protest to the Convention:

Citoyen-Président,

We have learned with regret that the National Convention has set a very short time within which the defense of Louis Capet is to be heard.

Allow us to inform you that it is physically impossible for two men, one more than sixty and the other more than seventy, to prepare, within so short a period, a defense against an accusation which comprises more than forty specific charges, in support of which there are one hundred and fifty-eight pieces of evidence of which most are not yet classified and some we have not yet had time to examine.

We have the greatest need of a third person to help us, and he whom we shall defend has selected Citoyen de Sèze, *homme de la loi,* of whose acceptance we are sure.

Malesherbes had desired to make a strong demand for a longer delay before the actual pleading of the case, but Louis XVI forbade them to ask for an extension of time. Malesherbes yielded the point, but only on condition that young De Sèze should be called in. Although the King did not know him personally, he had heard of his great ability, and he accepted the suggestion that De Sèze should deliver the plea. "Do it," said Louis XVI; "the physicians become more numerous as the danger increases. Your action shows me that the case is, indeed, a desperate one, but I shall show you that I know how to be a good patient."

As a matter of fact, Louis' explanation of this action of his two counselors was only partly correct. Malesherbes still believed that the King could be saved, but he felt that, because of their age and their frailty, neither he nor Tronchet would have the power of dominating so hostile a court as the Convention now appeared to be.

On the following day De Sèze joined them. The general outline of the defense had been already determined and drawn up, and De Sèze set himself to work on putting it into form for delivery. He was a past master at pleading, and Malesherbes had every confidence in him. But he felt that the work was progressing too slowly. He was always saying: "We must make haste, haste." The hours for consultation with the King remained the same, from five to nine in the evening, but the labors of the defense now extended into the early hours of the morning, long after they had left the Temple. Malesherbes, in his fear that they might be called to the bar of the Convention any day, was not so unreasonable as it would seem; almost every hour petitions were pouring in to the Convention demanding immediate action: "They are trying to divide the enemies of the throne; the monster of Royalism is reborn; he breathes vengeance; he regains his strength, and, while we waste time in discussing what to do with his remains, he meditates our death and his own resurrection." This from the section of Saint-Antoine in Paris. Others called on the "conscript fathers" to hear the "civicide Louis, le parjure," at once and be done with it.

Under such circumstances the work of preparing the

royal plea was carried on. Its writers were still hindered by the failure of the Convention to hand over all the papers that it had promised. Malesherbes undertook most of the negotiations with the committee. On December 21 and 22 he spent thirty-six hours in consultations which brought, finally, only a few more documents. During one of these expeditions he stopped at the Temple to speak to the King. He had with him a letter from the Convention absolving him from being searched. At the door he met Cubières, and showed him the order:

Cubières: "Your communication causes us a great deal of embarrassment; our responsibility is becoming an illusion; you can bring arms."

Malesherbes: "Usually I carry two knives; but I left them at home today. You may search me."

Cubières: "That the law forbids us to do."

Malesherbes: "In that case I shall search myself. . . . I have in my pocket papers about the Treaty of Pillnitz that concern the King."

Cubières: "You are an honest man, but if you were not you could bring the King arms or poison."

Malesherbes: "If the King had the religion of the philosophes, . . . if he were a Cato, he could kill himself. But the King is devout; he is a Catholic; he knows that his religion forbids it; . . . he will not destroy himself."

And he hurried out of the hall and up the stairs, the pockets of his greatcoat crammed with the precious papers.

Even the King took alarm at the constant comings and goings of Malesherbes, and he remonstrated with him: "Mon ami, why wear yourself out in this fashion? . . . I would prohibit these exertions but I know that you would

not obey me. At least, take more care of yourself. . . .
The sacrifice of my life has been made; save your own for
the sake of the family that adores you." But Malesherbes
would not heed him; he sped over Paris seeking more material and more evidence for De Sèze. At one time he even
considered trying to slip across the frontier to consult with
the émigrés. Second thought told him, however, that his
absence would be noted and that it might only increase the
rising tide of hostility against his client.

Finally the plea was in shape, and, on the late afternoon
of Christmas Day, 1792, at five o'clock Tronchet and Malesherbes met with the King to hear De Sèze read his oration.
They found Louis XVI ready for them, the table had been
placed near the small fire, and the only four chairs in the
room were drawn up to it. Malesherbes relates that Louis
followed the reading intently and interrupted the young
lawyer from time to time to ask a question or to make a
suggestion. At length the reading was over. There was a
deep silence, and then the King spoke: "Eloquent as it is,
Monsieur de Sèze, I must ask you to shorten your perora-
tion. It is not consistent with my dignity to have you evoke
such pity for my fate. I wish that you would make only a
brief and clear statement of the evidence that you offer in
my defense. What you omit, my dear De Sèze, will do me
less good than it might do you harm."

De Sèze was distressed by this remark, but he promised
to obey. He and Tronchet then retired and left Malesherbes alone with the King. "Let us talk for a little while
of other things," Louis XVI said. And he recalled, with a
smile, Malesherbes' aversion to the new fashions at the
Court and his dislike of elaborate dress. "Monsieur de Malesherbes," he said, "you and I have been ridiculed for hold-

ing to the customs of the old times, but is not that ridicule worth more than the beaux airs of today? Their varnish often conceals villainous things."

EARLY on the morning of December 27, the three lawyers met at the Temple. They found the streets lined with troops and before the Temple a strong guard had been drawn up. The sight of it recalled to Malesherbes the gardes d'honneur of other times. Louis XVI was ready and came down the stairs to join them but they were not allowed to accompany him. Surrounded by troops he made his short way to the meeting place of the Convention. There the King and his counselors met again and were ushered into an anteroom to await the pleasure of the tribunal. The King made several remarks to Malesherbes. To these Malesherbes replied, addressing Louis XVI, as was his wont, as Sire or Your Majesty. Treilhard, a deputy, overheard these expressions, and, putting himself between the King and his defender, said to Malesherbes: "What makes you so bold as to pronounce in this place titles that the Convention has forbidden?" The reply came quietly and firmly: "Mépris pour vous et mépris de la vie."

After a wait of nearly half an hour the group was admitted into the hall. The galleries were crowded with an audience that was said to have been carefully selected by the Jacobins and admitted the night before. The Convention was silent and dignified. The King walked quietly to the place assigned to him. He was perfectly composed and appeared to be in good health. An English observer remarks that the gallery had been very noisy but that it now became hushed and it seemed to have been affected by the appearance and dignity of the prisoner. The distinguished bearing of young De Sèze occasioned whispered comments of admiration, and as Malesherbes entered, his pallor and the set expression on his face caused some murmurs of sympathy. When the opening formalities had been observed, De Sèze was requested to make his plea. He began amid a silence so profound that he could be heard in the farthest corners of the gallery. The correct bearing of the Convention, an attitude which he had not anticipated, gave him courage: "Already the silence which I feel about me convinces me that a day of justice has succeeded to the days of anger and contention that have just passed, and that this solemn act which we now begin is not a mere form, that the temple of justice is indeed the abode of that impartiality which the law demands, and that any man who appears here before you stigmatized as an accused will receive the attention and interest even of those who accuse him. . . . Today, Messieurs, there is no power equal to yours, but there is one power which you do not have—you do not have the power to condemn unjustly."

From the moment that he uttered this challenge until he concluded his plea, the young lawyer held the rapt attention of his audience. In accordance with the expressed wish of Louis XVI, De Sèze did not challenge the competence of the Convention to judge the King. But, due to the insistence of Malesherbes, he was allowed to examine the limits to which that body could go in the matter of imposing a sentence. By an able examination of the laws of France he maintained that, while the Convention could

The Trial of Louis Sixteenth

From a contemporary engraving

pronounce on the guilt or innocence of the King, it had no power to decree any penalty other than that of dethronement and exile. The second part of the plea was devoted to the refutation of the forty-three accusations contained in the Acte énonciatif of December 11.

From the text of the plea it is perfectly clear what part of the oration was the work of Malesherbes and Tronchet and what part was that of De Sèze. The first section reproduces, in many instances, the style of the magistrate, the author of the Remonstrances of the Cour des Aides, while the refutation of the charges appears to have been written almost entirely by De Sèze. It is far more eloquent and dramatic—two characteristics for which the brilliant young lawyer from Bordeaux was already famed. Point by point, De Sèze refuted the accusations against Louis, and then he paused—to come to a sudden and unexpected close:

FRENCHMEN, the Revolution which regenerates you has wrought in you many virtues, but beware lest it destroy in your souls the sentiment of humanity. Without this, these virtues will be false.

Hear now, what History will relate in future times:

"Louis came to the throne at twenty years of age, and he set an example for us all; he was without culpable weakness or corrupting passion; he was economical, just, and severe; he showed himself to be the constant friend of the people. They desired the destruction of a ruinous taxation that was wearing them down; he destroyed it. They desired the abolition of serfdom; he began by abolishing it in his own domains. The people asked for a reform in criminal legislation and for the amelioration of the condition of those who were accused; he granted these reforms. The people wished for liberty and he gave it; he even anticipated it by personal sacrifices."

And, in spite of this, it is in the name of the people that you are demanding today . . .

Citizens, I shall not complete the sentence . . . I shall stop here before the verdict of history; know that history will judge your judgment and that her judgment will be the one to endure.

When De Sèze had ended, Louis was asked if he had anything to add. Briefly, he replied by confirming the statements of his defender, and then, in a louder tone, he concluded: "The charge that hurts me the most is the one that I have wished to shed the blood of my subjects. Against that assertion I protest with all my power."

The Convention then voted that the prisoner be returned to the Temple and resolved that it would confine its attention to the matter of a verdict to the exclusion of all other business. Accompanied by his counsel and the guards, Louis left the hall. It was about noon. "No disturbance of any kind occurred, and everything at this moment is perfectly quiet," a British agent reported to the home government. But within the hall of the Convention, pandemonium broke loose. Lanjuinais, Larivière, and, later, Vergniaud, Brissot, and Pétion demanded that whatever verdict was reached should be submitted to the nation. In the end their appeals were howled down by the gallery and their leaders, the Jacobins of the Mountain, who wished for the blood of the King.

What Malesherbes heard of these scenes convinced him that, in spite of the splendid effort of De Sèze, Louis would be convicted. But, unlike the King, he did not believe that the conventionnels would dare pronounce a sentence of death. He expected that deportation would be the penalty. In order to be prepared for this eventuality, he asked the King where he would prefer to go. Switzerland was the choice. "Suppose, Sire," said Malesherbes, "that the people of France called you back; would you return?" "If I followed my wishes, no; but duty would demand my return.

And even then I would come back only on two conditions: first, that the Catholic, Apostolic, and Roman religion should continue to be the religion of the State, without excluding the freedom of the other sects, and, again, that bankruptcy, if it was inevitable, should be acknowledged by those who have usurped the power." The King, who had already accepted death as his fate, changed the subject, and expressed his regret that he could not leave a legacy to his defenders. He added: "They would not allow you to have it anyhow; they would persecute you if you accepted it." As a matter of fact, Malesherbes knew that Louis XVI was practically penniless. On the eve of the trial, with considerable embarrassment, he had handed the King a purse: "Sire, allow a family that is rich partly through your kindness and that of your ancestors to make you this offering." The King had hesitated, but finally he had yielded to Malesherbes' instances. A little while after the trial, an official visited the Temple with orders to search everything in the room. In a drawer he found three small rolls. They were tied together and marked in the King's own hand—"Argent à rendre à Monsieur de Malesherbes." The rolls contained three thousand *livres d'or*. The money was confiscated . . .

During the long wait which followed the plea, Tronchet and De Sèze continued to follow the tempestuous debates in the Convention while Malesherbes devoted himself entirely to the King. He resumed his daily morning visits and continued to bring him the news. He brought him the latest plays to read. There was one of them that particularly delighted the King. It was a comedy that was being given at the Théâtre-Français and was called *L'Ami des Lois*. It was a veiled defense of Louis XVI. There was, in fact, after the first of the year, a general popular reaction in the King's favor. Agents of foreign governments bear witness to it in their reports. Malesherbes, ever the optimist, was encouraged by these signs, but Louis, Tronchet, and De Sèze believed that the effect of this reaction would be to provoke the Convention and make the extremists more than ever determined to force through a sentence of death.

For the moment, again, the King seemed indifferent to his own fate, and expressed great concern for that of his defenders. "One thing distresses me," Louis remarked to Malesherbes. "De Sèze and Tronchet owe me nothing, but they devote to me their time, their talents, and perhaps their lives; what return can I make for such services? If I made a bequest in their favor, it would not be carried out. Anyhow, it is not with money that such a debt can be discharged." "Sire," replied Malesherbes, "their own conscience and posterity will confer on them their just reward. But you may bestow one which will overpay them." "How?" asked the King. "Embrace them, Sire," answered Malesherbes.

As the debates in the Convention wore on, the conversations between the King and his former minister became more serious. Louis XVI seemed to be obsessed with the fate of Charles I of England, about whose fall he was now reading in Malesherbes' copy of Hume's *History*. The Stuarts and religion were now the principal topics of discussion between them. Once, near the end of the visit, the King very gently reproved his old friend for his earlier enthusiasms and his complete reliance on the philosophes. He had mentioned religion, and Malesherbes remained silent. Noticing the reticence of his companion, Louis continued: "Without religion, mon cher Malesherbes, there is no happiness for society or for the individual. Religion is the strongest bond between men; it prevents the abuse of power and of force, it protects the feeble, it consoles the unfortunate, and it guarantees, in the social order, the recognition of mutual obligations. Believe me, it is not possible to govern the people by the principles of philosophy alone."

This remark must have struck home, although the old gentleman when he related the incident did not comment on its application to himself. Instead, he added: "This conviction was in Louis XVI the solid basis of all his virtues; it made him a King, just, clement, humane, and benevolent; it made him a faithful husband, a good father, and a considerate master; in a word, a model of moral and domestic virtues."

This was Malesherbes' final estimate of the character and abilities of Louis XVI. It was delivered when he himself was a prisoner. Its inclusions are significant and its omissions are characteristic of his honesty and good faith.

By the evening of January 16 it was evident that the Convention was determined upon the destruction of the King. Tronchet and De Sèze then urged their colleague to wait no longer but to inform the King of his impending fate. At nine o'clock on the following morning Malesherbes appeared at the Temple. Cléry met him at the door, and Malesherbes whispered to him: "Tout est perdu, le roi est condamné." Louis heard him enter, arose from the table

at which he had been seated, and came forward to meet
him. Malesherbes knelt before him and told him of the
likelihood of an unfavorable verdict. The King evinced
not the slightest surprise; he bent over and helped Malesherbes to rise. They went together into his cabinet.

For some time the King and his counselor had been discussing the matter of his religious duties. The time had
now come when Louis must have the consolations of the
Church. He asked Malesherbes to search out for him the
Abbé Edgeworth de Firmont and, as a last favor, to obtain
the consent of the Convention for the abbé to minister to
him. He added: "This is a strange commission for such a
philosophe as I know you to be; but if you had suffered as
much as I have, and were about to die, as I am, I should
wish you to enjoy those religious sentiments which would
support you and console you much more than philosophy.
My dear Monsieur de Malesherbes, it is with all my heart
that I pray God to enlighten you." At once the old man
set out on this mission. He located the abbé and met him
at the house of Madame de Senozan. There it was arranged
that, once permission had been granted, the abbé would
confess and communicate the King.

Malesherbes' compliance, however, did not mean that
he had abandoned all hope of saving the life of his royal
client. There was still a desperate measure to be attempted
—he and the other defenders were resolved to demand
that the verdict be submitted to the nation. The King had
no faith in the success of such a venture, but he gave his
consent. At Malesherbes' request he had written out some
time previously a declaration which he now handed to
him: "I owe it to my own honor and to that of my family
to refuse to accept the judgment convicting me of a crime

for which I cannot reproach myself. Consequently, I demand that this verdict of its representatives be submitted to the nation. By this act I give power to my defenders and I require of their loyalty that they inform the Convention of my appeal and that this appeal be recorded in the minutes of the Convention."

Armed with this document the counsel went on January 17 to the Convention and demanded a special hearing. Their request was granted reluctantly. De Sèze read the act and argued that the appeal of the King could not be denied on the ground that the Convention had voted not to submit their decree to the nation. The appeal, he said, was the right of the accused. "I demand it of you in the name of justice, in the name of the *patrie,* in the name of humanity. Do not give to France and to Europe the horrible spectacle of a decree of death voted by a majority of five in your body." Tronchet spoke briefly. Then came the turn of Malesherbes. Emotion overcame him; he spoke in broken sentences and could hardly be heard: "When I was a magistrate and again since that time, I have often reflected on this question—in a case of crime how many votes should be necessary for a condemnation—allow me to put these considerations on paper. I am no longer used to speaking in public—I beg of you to let me have until tomorrow to present them to you."

His request was denied, and the King's appeal was rejected. President Vergniaud brought their audience to an end with the following words: "Citizens, the National Convention has heard your pleas. It was your sacred duty to make them, since you were charged with the defense of Louis. *La Convention vous accorde les honneurs de la séance.*" Later, with remorse Malesherbes wrote: "My colleagues spoke well, but my performance was bad, because in place of reasons I could find only tears."

Defeated, the three retired. On the street they were met by a handful of Royalists who came up to Malesherbes and told him that they would attempt a rescue of the King. The defenders hastened back to the Temple, where Malesherbes informed the King of the plot, but Louis XVI, much agitated, commanded him to put a stop to it. Too much blood had been shed already, he said. Tronchet and De Sèze took their leave, and Malesherbes was left alone with his master. There was a moment of silence, and then one of the guard that since the previous day had always been in the room stepped up to Malesherbes and said he would leave them for a little while. There is no record of what passed between the two men when the guard withdrew into the corridor, except that Malesherbes told the King that his confessor would be allowed to come to him. In a few minutes Louis XVI and his minister appeared at the door; Louis was leading Malesherbes by the hand: "A happier future will bring us together again. I hate to leave such a friend. Adieu, come back early this evening; I need to see you often in these difficult hours. Adieu, adieu." And Malesherbes records: "Je sortis du Temple, le coeur brisé."

Later that evening he returned. At the foot of the stairs he was stopped by a guard who told him that an order had come forbidding him to see the King again.

On January 21 the Abbé Edgeworth de Firmont accompanied Louis XVI to the place of execution and stayed with him to the end. Then, at the lifting of the King's head and the triumphant cry of "Vive la République!" he fled from the scaffold and fought his way through the lines of troops and the milling crowds to Malesherbes' residence. There the old man embraced the priest and cried: "Tout est fini. Receive my everlasting thanks and those of all worthy Frenchmen for the fidelity which you have shown to our good master."

CHAPTER X

REVOLUTIONARY TRIBUNAL
AND GUILLOTINE

IT had been Malesherbes' intention to leave for his estate as soon as the decree of the Convention had been fulfilled and Louis XVI had paid at the guillotine the penalty of his failings. But his friends insisted that he remain in Paris. They believed that he would be more secure there. As one who had been a defender of the King, he was now a marked man, and, they argued, in the provinces he would be more conspicuous than in Paris. In the capital, they said, he could more quickly regain the obscurity that was necessary for his safety. Although he did not wish to do so, his family persuaded him to follow this advice, and he remained quietly in Paris until the agitation for the trial of Marie Antoinette began. Then, fearful that the Queen would feel obliged to require his services and knowing that he was too feeble to undertake her defense, he retired to Malesherbes. There, while Robespierre and the Terrorists turned on the Girondists and began hacking their way to power, Malesherbes remained in seclusion.

In his retreat he was accompanied by his daughter, Madame de Rosambo; her husband; his granddaughter, Madame de Chateaubriand; and Monsieur de Chateaubriand, brother of the famous writer. "We are faced with many dangers," wrote Madame de Rosambo, "but I think that the good name of my father will protect us all. His name is sacred, even among our enemies." His family continued to stay there with him, watching over the parent who had become almost a cult.

But the truth was that by the spring of 1793, Malesherbes' position in public opinion had become almost reversed. Where before he had been regarded as a benign friend of the Revolution and had often been adopted by the Extremists without his consent, now that fact was nearly forgotten. When people thought of him at all, it was not as the magistrate who had loved liberty and the companion of Turgot who had fought for reform, but as the old nobleman who had spent most of his remaining talents in an effort to save the King. He was no longer suspected by the Royalists; he was revered by them, and, for those who were still in France, his house was almost a shrine.

His children and grandchildren were partly responsible for this metamorphosis. No one of them had followed him the whole way in his enthusiasms for liberty. During part of the year 1792, Madame de Rosambo had been an émigrée in enemy countries, and, in May, there had been some correspondence about the advisability of moving the old gentleman across the frontier to Colmar. Both his daughter and her children had carried on correspondence with their emigrant friends. In the opinion of those in power it mattered not if, as Madame de Rosambo later asserted, she had ceased to write her letters when the law forbade correspondence with those who had not returned. Her husband, likewise, had been out of the country. Once he had sojourned briefly in Lausanne and, later, in Milan. A more active member of the family had been Jean Baptiste de Chateaubriand, the son-in-law of Rosambo, who traveled

in Belgium and in England and who, it appears, kept up
a steady correspondence with a number of émigrés. But
the most active of them all seems to have been Madame de
Senozan, Malesherbes' sister, who was undoubtedly concerned in the petty conspiracies of Valence, and who, until
the autumn of 1792, kept in close contact with developments at Colmar.

The house of Malesherbes was becoming suspect, and
it was destined to be drawn into the net which Robespierre
and the Jacobins were spreading for all aristocrats, whether
they were aristocrats by birth or merely by sentiment. The
fact that there was not enough evidence to convict counted
for little; there was sufficient evidence to suspect. And suspicion began to attach itself to the father as well as to the
children.

As a matter of fact, once the King's plea had failed,
Malesherbes was not strong enough to do any harm; nor
was he of a mind to do so if he could. He was frail, half
blind, and weary; he spent most of his time pottering
about his gardens. He tried to forget the tragedy of the
King, and complained that he could not do so. He knew
that, in this later hour of liberty, his idea of liberty was an
anachronism. The age of the philosophes had passed, and
Malesherbes' idea of liberty had been theirs. He had not
stood for a liberty which would force and bind. The liberty that he knew did not require laws to guarantee it; it
had no need of responsible ministries or limited monarchies. It had nothing to do with guillotines and committees of public safety. The sort of liberty for which he
had fought was one that would come from the reform of
abuses and a complete harmony between an all-powerful

king and a National Assembly. It reposed on that fundamental gospel of the eighteenth century—the inherent goodness of man. Malesherbes' approach to the problem had been a scholastic and idealistic one; he had not been a practical or realistic advocate.

This is not entirely conjecture. There is only one statement of his that survives from this period, but it proves the point: "Turgot and I were terribly honest men with a passion for good. We knew mankind only from books. Without knowing it and without wishing it, we contributed to the Revolution."

This is Malesherbes' condemnation of himself. It was made about the time when the climax of the Revolution was reached and the Constitution of the Terror was accepted. Then it was that he saw clearly his own mistake. Then he found himself living in a strange land which was, in part, his own creation and yet was inimical to him.

In December, 1793, the Committee of Public Safety, with its subsidiary bodies, became in practice the supreme authority in France. Its rule was known as the Terror. But in the minds of its founders it was purely a temporary and defensive measure to create in France a power that would drive back the foreign allies and purge France of the remaining adherents of the ancien régime. War to the death and extermination of the *défaitistes* within the country became the immediate purposes of the body which established its domination over the Convention.

Hardly had this latest regime come into being than
Malesherbes' residence in the Quartier du Marais in Paris
was searched. This action had probably been precipitated
by the arrest of one Monsieur Hell, a member of the former Constituent Assembly and a protégé of the family,
who, on 29 Germinal, had been summoned before the Tribunal. The charge was "correspondence and maneuvers
tending to calumniate the people and to vilify national
representation and liberty." Papers which were discovered
at his house included some letters from the rather indis-
creet Madame de Senozan. These, together with all the
papers seized at the residence of Malesherbes, were taken
to the Revolutionary Tribunal and examined there. Contrary to the usual procedure Fouquier-Tinville's signature
or else his initials appear on almost every bit of written evidence which was later produced against the family.* The
most incriminating evidence was a series of letters of Monsieur Hell to Madame de Senozan. These last indicated
quite clearly that she and her correspondent were impli-
cated in fomenting opposition in the country and were in
direct communication with the enemies on the Rhine.

Nothing was known at Malesherbes of the seizure until
one morning in December when the owner, who was
walking in his garden, saw the officers of the neighboring
town coming up his lane. They were headed by three
rather ferocious looking gentlemen who carried swords.
The three strangers were emissaries from the great committee in Paris, and they had come to arrest Monsieur and

* The *Dossier Malesherbes* contained sixty letters of young Chateaubriand
and the correspondence of Madame de Rosambo as well as letters from various
émigrés to Malesherbes complaining of their unhappy state and letters from
relatives who had left France, thanking him for money which he had sent
them.

Madame de Rosambo. Malesherbes was left with his grandchildren.

Early on the following day a second delegation arrived with orders for Malesherbes and the remaining members of his household to go with them.* The old gentleman and his companions complied without protest, but before they set out the local officials had the grace to ask that Malesherbes should be allowed to proceed without the humiliation of an armed guard. By night time the party had arrived at the outskirts of Paris and was lodged in the prison of Madelonettes. Malesherbes immediately petitioned that all the family be placed in the same prison. His request was granted, and, two days later, the entire family was reunited at the prison of Port-Royal, which had been renamed ironically Portes-Libres.

During the first few days of his captivity Malesherbes appeared to have been considerably shocked by this unexpected arrest of his family. His unconquerable optimism had led him to believe, at first, that the misfortunes which had come to himself and his relatives would be momentary and that a demand from him for immediate investigation would be complied with at once. When no reply to these demands came, he was perplexed and troubled. But once the family were all together at Portes-Libres, his natural gaiety returned. He is said to have regaled the distinguished company every evening with anecdotes and to have organized and participated in charades and games. While in this prison he met many of his former acquaintances. Among them he encountered Monsieur Hue, valet

---

* This group included the Chateaubriands, Monsieur and Madame de Tocqueville, another daughter and son-in-law of the Rosambos, and Dubois, the tutor, and his wife.

to Louis XVI. To him he related his experiences during the imprisonment and trial of the King, and he gave him a brief account of what had happened.*

Almost every day some of the company in the Portes-Libres were called out to appear before the Revolutionary Tribunal. Few of these ever returned. For several weeks the family of Malesherbes remained undisturbed; Robespierre and his satellites were occupied with the incrimination and destruction of Hébert and his followers, and then came Danton's turn. It was not until April that the first break came, when Rosambo was removed to the prison of St. Pélagie. This event aroused Malesherbes to action. He appealed by letter to each member of the Tribunal for Rosambo, and, at the same time, he addressed to the Convention a demand that he be informed of the reasons for the imprisonment of himself and the other members of his family. To both communications there was, at first, no reply, and no word was received of Rosambo. Malesherbes and his children were left in suspense until the morning of April 20, when, as was the custom, the guard called out in the corridor the roll of those who had been guillotined. Among the names was Rosambo.

Only a few hours later, Malesherbes and his family were removed to the Conciergerie. This prison was now known as the antechamber of the guillotine. By this time Malesherbes had been informed of the accusations against him. They had been drawn up by Fouquier-Tinville himself a month before, but the struggle with Danton had probably

---

* Later Hue published this account in his own *Recollections*. Most of its contents are verified by consultation of other journals and notes, notably those of Cléry and of the Abbé Morellet, who was, for a time, imprisoned with Malesherbes and to whom Malesherbes talked, after telling him that he had written a memoir which he finally decided to burn.

been responsible for the delay. Malesherbes found himself accused of conspiracy, of sending funds out of the country, and of wishing a bad season for the vines so that the French people would suffer. But the principal charge was the fact that, as an aristocrat, he had defended the King: "Lamoignon Malesherbes presents all the appearances of a conspirator and a counterrevolutionary. The documents that have been found at this magistrate's house prove that he was constantly occupied in an effort to bring back the old order of things and that he was the center about which the other conspirators, who have already been brought to justice, rallied, and that he directed all their activities. One can only regard him as the person who advised the infamous protestations against the sovereignty of the people. His correspondence further establishes the fact that the offer which he made to defend Capet, an offer which Capet accepted, was only the result of an intrigue of Pitt's cabinet with the relations of Malesherbes who had emigrated to London, and that in this role of defender he was simply the agent of all the counterrevolutionaries who were subsidized by the despot of England. Finally, the letters which have been found prove that he kept in correspondence with the enemies of the State, notably with his children, to whom he sent funds and whose return to France he facilitated, and with My Lord Richmond."

When he was confronted with these charges, Malesherbes denied them all and remarked to a friend who stood near him: "Surely they could have put a little more semblance of truth into them."

Most of the accusations were too foolish to be taken seriously. By April, 1794, the charge of conspiracy with Pitt had become a cliché in the Revolutionary Tribunal, and the letters included in the evidence give not the slightest reasonable indication of any counterrevolutionary activity on the part of Malesherbes. A number of these letters were written by Madame de Rosambo to her father while she was an émigrée. Many of them were concerned with his interests in botany. They contained technical terms which apparently perplexed the investigators and aroused their suspicions, for they have been underscored in red ink by the inquisitors. A careful examination of these letters shows that there is no possibility of a code.

There remained, however, the letters of the émigrés addressed to Madame de Senozan, to Madame de Rosambo, and to her children. The nature of these epistles aroused a suspicion which attached itself to Malesherbes as well as to his family.

The interrogation of Malesherbes was brief, and his replies were monosyllabic. He denied all the charges. He did not care to prolong the ordeal; he was old and through with life, and eager to be gone from a world which he did not comprehend. He accepted whatever defense they offered to him, for he knew from experience what a farce the whole procedure would be. He offered his defender no information or advice. He was eager for his sentence, and, when it came, he accepted it gladly. Even the condemnation of his daughter and his grandchildren did not distress him greatly. Rosambo had preceded them yesterday; they would follow him today. And when the summons came, gallantly he offered his arm to his daughter. But this gesture was spoiled when they bound his hands. Followed by Monsieur and Madame de Chateaubriand and a company of thirty others, the two walked to the tumbrils that were to take them to the guillotine. The old gentleman's sight was bad, and, as he passed beneath the door, he stumbled over the doorsill. "That is what they call an evil omen," he remarked. "A Roman, if he were in my place, would go no further." Arrived at the guillotine, he stood on the steps while, one by one, his daughter, his granddaughter, and Monsieur de Chateaubriand preceded him.

BIBLIOGRAPHICAL NOTE

THIS study of Malesherbes has been based primarily on documents in the archives of the Tocqueville family. This collection contains a great number of unpublished letters, miscellaneous notes and manuscripts, and published brochures of Chrétien de Malesherbes. Among them are his unpublished *Memoir on the Nobles, Memoir on the Present Situation,* and the important *Memoirs on Religious Toleration.* There are also a quantity of letters addressed to him from Turgot, Marquis de Mirabeau, Boissy d'Anglas, Rabaut Saint-Étienne, and other prominent people of the period. The entire manuscript of his famous *Herbier* is also there. In the archives of Chateaurenard, now in the possession of the family of Madame de Virel, there are a series of letters of Malesherbes to various friends and relatives and his unpublished commentary on Montesquieu. These important documents have been consulted. I have also used information from the papers of Monsieur De Sèze, who delivered the plea for Louis XVI.

Recently I acquired a collection of unpublished Malesherbes' manuscripts of considerable importance. These include three letters of Malesherbes to Monsieur de Boisegibault relating to the difficulties of the Cour des Aides, correspondence with Monsieur Thouin, director of the Jardin des Plantes, two discourses written in 1787 and 1789, both unpublished, and also a manuscript containing an account of the last conversation of Malesherbes with Louis XVI. This manuscript is either a copy of or possibly the original source for the accounts given by Monsieur Hue and Monsieur Dubois. There are also copies of letters of Malesherbes to the two other defenders of the King.

In the Archives Nationales at Paris, the dossier of the Revolutionary Tribunal, the trial of Louis XVI, the trial of Malesherbes and his family, the dossiers of the Conseil général de la commune de Paris and of the Conseil exécutif provisoire de la Convention, and the Archives et registres de la Cour des Aides have been consulted. The Bibliothèque Nationale possesses a remarkable collection of the correspondence and decrees of the Department of the

Librairie and Imprimerie. These are of great importance for the study of Malesherbes as censor. I have also used the *Moniteur*, the *Journal des débats et des décrets de la Convention*, and other Paris newspapers of the time. The British Museum has in its possession the journal of Bertrand de Moleville, a friend of Malesherbes and an émigré who remained closely in touch with affairs in France in 1792–93. Bertrand's *Journal* should be used with caution. In addition I have had access to the letters of the British foreign agents in Paris, now to be found in the Public Records Office, which were communicated to me by Mr. William B. Willcox.

There is a mass of nearly contemporary material relative to Malesherbes during the Revolution. Of these works I have used the following as the most reliable:

1) Jean Baptiste Cléry—*Journal de ce qui s'est passé à la tour du Temple pendant la captivité de Louis XVI, roi de France*. Cléry was valet-de-chambre to the King and remained with him in the Temple during the trial. The *Journal* was compiled by Cléry from notes taken by him at the time. It was first published in London in 1798.

2) François Hue—*Dernières années du règne et de la vie de Louis XVI*. Hue was likewise valet-de-chambre to the Dauphin and to the King. He was allowed to remain with Louis XVI almost to the last. This memoir was compiled by Hue from notes taken in the Temple while he was with the King. Later Hue found himself a fellow prisoner with Malesherbes at the Portes-Libres, where Malesherbes reviewed with him their past experiences and dictated to him an account of the events relating to Louis XVI and to his conversations with the King. Hue's work was first published in 1806 in London. There appears to be no copy of the original edition extant. A second edition was published in Paris in 1814. This edition is generally accepted as a careful reproduction of the first. Cléry's and Hue's narratives contain considerable detail concerning conversations between Malesherbes and his client. Their narratives correspond to the manuscript in my possession, and are further corroborated by the account of Dubois, the tutor to the family of Malesherbes. I have drawn on these sources, in great part, for sections of Chapter IX.

3) Marie Thérèse Charlotte de France (Madame d'Angoulême)—*Mémoires*. This small volume was completed in the Temple on October 14, 1795. It was first published at Montpellier in 1817.

4) Jean François Lepitre—*Souvenirs et notes fidèles sur mon service au Temple depuis 8 décembre 1792 jusqu'au 26 mars 1793*. Lepitre, formerly a professor of rhetoric at the University of Paris, was a *commissaire* of the Convention at the Temple. The *Souvenirs* were first published at Paris in 1817.

5) Henry Essex Edgeworth de Firmont—*Relation des derniers moments de Louis XVI*. Abbé Edgeworth de Firmont was the priest who confessed Louis XVI and accompanied him to the scaffold. The *Relation* was first published in Paris in 1817.

There are no authentic biographies of Malesherbes. The first *notice* was published anonymously in 1802 under the title of *Malesherbiana*. The author was probably Cousin d'Avallon. Other later accounts by Boissy d'Anglas, Dubois, Mangin, Gaillard, and Vignaux are purely eulogistic. Jean Baptiste Dubois, who was named by Malesherbes to be tutor to his grandson, Louis le Pelletier de Rosambo, mentions a manuscript of memoirs by Malesherbes which was destroyed and of which he quotes what he claims to be a fragment. In 1927 the late Henri Robert published a brilliant monograph on Malesherbes, but it is obviously based on the preceding accounts, and it contains certain errors which are misleading as far as an interpretation of Malesherbes is concerned. It is my understanding that, in the future, a biography will be written by the Vicomte de Rosambo, one of the descendants of Malesherbes.

There are a quantity of important references to Malesherbes in the better-known published letters and memoirs of the period. Of these the more valuable, for this subject, are the writings of Madame du Deffand, the Abbé Morellet, Horace Walpole, David Hume, Marquis d'Argenson, Comte d'Argenteau, Bachaumont, Condorcet, Rousseau, Voltaire, Diderot, d'Alembert, Rivarol, and Mercier's *Tableau de Paris* and the *Correspondance Metra*. Turgot's papers, which appear to have been edited in toto by Schelles, are very useful. I have also been able to acquire and use a very valuable and little-known work entitled *Mémoires pour servir à l'histoire du droit public de la France en matière d'impôts, ou Recueil de ce qui s'est passé à la Cour des Aides, depuis 1756 jusqu'au mois de juin 1775.* This work was published in 1779 and was suppressed by decree of the Cour des Aides in February of that year. By some authorities the authorship is attributed to Malesherbes.

Few of the recognized standard works and biographies of the eighteenth century and of the Revolution give much information about Malesherbes, although all of them acknowledge his importance. These have been carefully examined. Flammeront's *Histoire des Parlements* is an invaluable work and little known today. *Captivité et derniers moments de Louis XVI* in two volumes, published in 1892 by the Marquis de Beaucourt for the Société de l'Histoire Contemporaine, is a useful and reliable guide. In 1936 a life of Monsieur de Sèze and an analysis of the plea was brought out by the Abbé Sevin. This work sheds little light on the part played by Malesherbes and is concerned exclusively with the young De Sèze and his activities. There is an amusing interpretation of Malesherbes in Pierre Gaxotte's *Louis XV et son temps.*

INDEX

112, 117, 119–120, 122–125, 126, 127, 128–129, 131, 132, 137; conversations with Malesherbes in the Temple, 138–141, 143–144, 145–147, 150–153, 154–156; trial and execution, 137–157
Luxembourg, Duc and Duchesse de, 38

MALESHERBES, Chrétien Guillaume de Lamoignon de, birth, 4; youth and education, 4–6, 13; marriage, 12, 106–107; Director of the Librairie, 11–31; and Voltaire, 21, 29, 31; and Diderot, 23, 24–29; and Helvetius, 23–24; and d'Alembert, 24–28, 35, 75, 83; and the Encyclopedia, 24–29; and Rousseau, 32–42, 107; and Montesquieu, 13, 14, 26, 30, 66–67; botanist, 17–18, 41, 72–73, 105, 106, 109; and the Church, 14–15, 50, 94–97, 116–118, 130; First President of the Cour des Aides, 43–65, 77–82; and Turgot, 40–41, 43, 73, 79–81, 82, 83, 86, 87–88, 94–98, 100, 101, 103–104, 107–108; as Minister, 81–104, 116–120; election to the Academy, 84–86; defense of the King, 137–157; trial and execution, 158–167
Malesherbes, ideas of, on Estates-General, 62, 69–70, 97, 114, 120, 121–126; on lettres de cachet, 51, 55–56, 57–58, 71, 90–94, 126; on liberty of the press, 18–29, 31, 86; on monarchy, 15–16, 29, 30, 68–70, 71, 78–79, 85, 86, 97–98, 100–101, 122, 124, 125, 160, 161; on religion, 13, 14–15, 30–31, 94–97, 117–118, 126, 130, 152–153, 154; on taxation, 48–51, 80, 124, 126
Maria Theresa, 46, 75, 83
Marie Antoinette, Queen of France, 74, 75, 87, 88, 102–103, 104, 132, 140, 158
Martinière, La, 88
Maupeou, René Nicolas, 51, 52–53, 54, 55, 56–57, 58–61, 63–64, 71, 74–75, 76
Maurepas, Count Frédéric de, 75, 76, 77, 80, 83, 86, 91, 93, 103, 112, 113, 139
Mazarin, Cardinal, 2
Mercy-Argenteau, Count de, 83, 88
Moleville, Bertrand de, 102, 128–129, 137, 142
Monnerat, Affaire, 55–56
Montesquieu, Charles de Secondat, Baron de, 9, 13, 14, 16, 25, 26, 30, 66–67, 69, 71
Montgolfier, Joseph and Étienne, 110
Morellet, André, Abbé de, 24, 25, 28, 62–63, 109, 141, 164

NATIONAL ASSEMBLY, 127, 128, 139
Necker, Jacques, 110, 112–114, 120
Neufchâteau, François de, 133
Newton, Sir Isaac, 10, 13, 26

ORLÉANS, Louis Philippe Joseph, Duc de, 2–3, 21, 77
Orléans, Duchesse de, 24
Ossory, Countess, 89

PAINE, Thomas, 130
   Pétion, Jerôme, 150
Pitt, William, 165–166
Pompadour, Marquise de, 25, 28, 37, 51
Prades, Abbé de, 26
Pucelle, Abbé, 4

QUESNAY, François, 25

RABAUT SAINT-ÉTIENNE, Jean Paul, 95, 117, 122, 126
   Réaumur, René de, 16
Rey, Marc Michel, 34, 36
Reynière, Marie Françoise Grimaud de la (Mme. Malesherbes), 12, 106–107
Richelieu, Cardinal de, 43
Robespierre, Maximilian, 133–134, 158, 160, 164, 166
Roland, Jean Marie, 130, 131
Rosambo, Marie Antoinette, Mme. de, 108–109, 158–159, 162–163, 166–167
Rosambo, Paul de, 123–124, 126, 158, 159, 162–163, 164, 166
Rousseau, Jean Jacques, 25, 32–42, 107, 124

SAINT-GERMAIN, Claude Louis, Comte de, 83, 100
   Saint-Maur, Dupré de, 84, 85
Saint-Pierre, Abbé de, 8, 13
Sallay, 35
Séguier, 103
Senozan, Mme. de, 154, 160, 162
Sèze, Romain de, 143–144, 146, 147, 148–150, 151, 152, 153, 155, 156
Sieyès, Emmanuel-Joseph, Abbé, 121

TARGET, 135
   Tennis Court Oath, 127, 128
Terray, Abbé, 56, 59, 74
Tocqueville, M. and Mme., 163
Treilhard, Jean Baptiste, 147
Tronchet, François Denis, 135–136, 138–139, 141, 142–143, 144, 146, 147, 149, 151, 152, 155, 156
Turgot, Anne Robert Jacques, 5, 25, 35, 40–41, 43, 73–74, 75, 76–77, 79–80, 81, 82, 83, 84, 86, 87, 90, 94–100, 101, 103–104, 107–108, 113, 122, 159, 161

VAUBAN, 6, 7
   Vergennes, Charles Gravier, Comte de, 75
Vergniaud, Pierre Victurnien, 150, 155

Villegagnon, Mme. de, 89
Voltaire, François Arouet de, 21, 25, 27, 29, 31, 33, 34–35, 40, 46, 75–76
Vrillière, Duc de la, 63–64, 81, 83, 90–91

WALPOLE, HORACE, 79, 81, 83, 89–90, 91, 104
Walpole, Robert, 8
Wittenbach, Pastor, 106

Date Due